CORSICA

Alalia

ETRURIA

• Alba Fucentia

R. Tiber

• Rome

• Praeneste
(Palestrina)

• Ostia

LATIUM

SAMNIUM

Cumae
(Naples)
Puteoli
Misenum
Pompeii

(Ruvo) •

• Brundisium

• Tarentum

LUCANIA

SARDINIA

TYRRHENIAN SEA

BRUTTIUM

Croton •

LIPARI
ISLANDS

AEGATES
ISLANDS

Drepana

Mylae •

Panormus

Tyndaris
Messana

• Rhegium

Segesta

Tauromenium

Himera

Naxos

Lilybaeum
(Marsala)

Mt. Aetna

SICILY

Catana •

Agrigentum

Syracuse •

Cape
Ecnomus

• Gela

Utica •

Carthage •
(Tunis)

• (Tébessa)

Themetra • (Sousse)

MALTA

Rome

Hadrumetum

Mahdia •

0   100 miles

Thapsus •

(front cover) Partly uncovered hull of a
Roman merchantman of about 60–65 BC
with estimated dimensions of 30–35 m
long and 9 m broad and burthen 300–
400 tons. Photo: by permission of
M.P-M.Duval, Director of the *Revue
Gallia* in *supplément xxxive* where
the photograph appears, and of M.Ph.
Foliot of the Centre Camille Jullian,
Centre National de Recherche
Scientifique, University of Provence.
Cliché CNRS Chéné.

(back cover) Detail of the mosaic in the
Palazzo Barberini at Palestrina. Early
1st century BC. Photo: Vasari

© Crown copyright 1980
First published 1980
ISBN 0 11 290311 8
Design by HMSO Graphic Design
Printed in England for
Her Majesty's Stationery Office
by W. S. Cowell Ltd, Ipswich
Dd 587538   K160

National Maritime Museum

THE SHIP

Long Ships and Round Ships
Warfare and Trade in the Mediterranean
3000 BC–500 AD

John Morrison

London
Her Majesty's Stationery Office

Contents

The author's thanks are due to Professor John Crook of St John's College, Cambridge, who kindly read the text in manuscript and drew attention to a number of errors. Professor Crook is not responsible for those that remain.

(below) Mosaic in the Baths at Themetra (nr Sousse, Tunisia). About the middle of the 3rd century AD. After L.Foucher, *Navires et Barques, etc.* Notes et Documents XV. Institut National d'Archéologie et Arts, Tunis, 1957. fig.9.

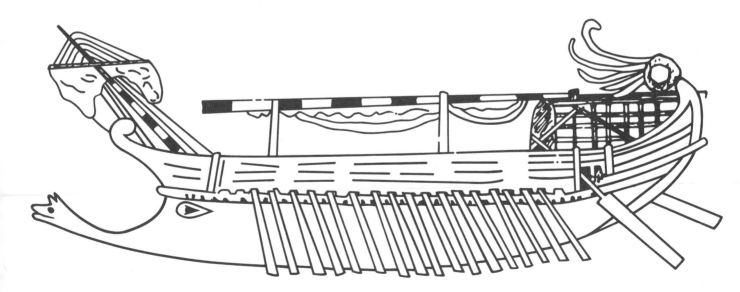

Introduction by the General Editor

This is the second of a series of ten short books on the development of the ship, both the merchant vessel and the specialized vessel of war, from the earliest times to the present day, commissioned and produced jointly by the National Maritime Museum and Her Majesty's Stationery Office.

The books are each self-contained, each dealing with one aspect of the subject, but together they cover the evolution of vessels in terms which are detailed, accurate and up-to-date. They incorporate the latest available information and the latest thinking on the subject, but they are readily intelligible to the non-specialist, professional historian or layman.

Above all, as should be expected from the only large and comprehensive general historical museum in the world which deals especially with the impact of the sea on the development of human culture and civilization, the approach is unromantic and realistic. Merchant ships were and are machines for carrying cargo profitably. They carried the trade and, in the words of the very distinguished author of this second book, 'the creation of wealth through trade is at the root of political and military power'. The vessel of war, the maritime vehicle of that power, follows and she is a machine for men to fight from, or with.

It follows from such an approach that the illustrations to the series are for the most part from contemporary sources. The reader can form his own conclusions from the evidence, written and visual. We have not commissioned hypothetical reconstructions, the annotation of which, done properly, would take up quite a percentage of the text.

In this second book of the series, Mr Morrison deals with the development of ships in southern Europe from the earliest times of which there is any record to 500 AD. The bulk of the evidence is literary and iconographic, though there is some archaeological evidence of ship structures. Most of the literary evidence comes from official sources or from the writings of contemporary or near contemporary writers and is therefore concerned with official ships financed at public expense, that is warships, and the bulk of the text therefore deals with these vessels.

The period covered goes only to the dawn of sailing in the later sense of the term and the principal method of propulsion of the vessels described was rowing with oars at a maximum of three levels. Rowing is almost totally out of fashion in Britain today as a means of propulsion of any kind of boat, though on both coasts of North America and on many inland waters in that continent the use of traditional and often finely built rowing boats is again coming into its own as a form of exercise and relaxation. Though the development of sailing with suitable boats released men from much drudgery, rowing as a means of propulsion of boats and small vessels was very widespread until the development of small internal combusion engines early in the present century. There were many environments in which rowing was an altogether more practical means of propulsion than sail, on great rivers, in estuaries, in narrow waters, in areas of predictable weather, and even in some inshore fisheries.

In his last chapter, Mr Morrison describes the structures of some of the vessels with which he has dealt as far as is possible on the basis of the available evidence. The really important thing is that these boats and vessels were constructed by building a shell of planks joined together at their edges and into this shell were inserted strengthening frames shaped to fit the shell. In fact, edge-joined shell construction, one small possible hint from Herodotus apart, was the usual method of building vessels in the period covered in this book. The systems used were perhaps very different from those of the late North European edge-joined boatbuilding traditions described in the first volume in this series. The edge-joining in some Southern European traditions may have played a

smaller part in the total strength of the vessel than it did in North Europe. A large part of the general strength may have come from the wales, the massive strakes relatively high in the structure. But the vessel was nevertheless constructed as a shell into which frames, shaped to fit, were inserted.

It is important to emphasise this point because for generations scholars have assumed that the vessels of the classical world were built like 19th century wooden ships, by first erecting a skeleton of frames and then covering it with a skin of planks which were not joined to one another at the edges. We know now that this technique of shipbuilding, which enabled much bigger, stronger and more seaworthy vessels to be built, did not develop generally until much later – perhaps as late as the 1200s or even the 1300s. The origin and age of the technique are still unknown and unclear, but its adoption enable western man to develop the three-masted sailing ship and with this vehicle he was able to explore and dominate the oceans of the world. Dr McGowan will be summarizing briefly the present state of knowledge on this fascinating problem in the appropriate later volume of this series.

Mr Morrison is one of the two leading authorities in the world on the development of ships in southern Europe during the period he covers. A distinguished classical scholar, President of Wolfson College, Cambridge, he has interested himself in the subject for over forty years and his book *Greek Oared Ships*, written with R.T.Williams, is the standard work of its kind.

Basil Greenhill
DIRECTOR, NATIONAL MARITIME MUSEUM
General Editor

Drawing of a mosaic from the Baths at Themetra showing a Roman round ship of the 3rd century AD. From L.Foucher, *Navires et Barques, etc.*

Chronological table

Select bibliography

L. Basch 'Phoenician Oared Ships' *Mariner's Mirror* 55 (1969) 2 and 3 = Basch (1969)

G. F. Bass 'Cape Gelidonya etc' *Trans. Am. Phil. Soc.* NS 57 (1967) iv; *The History of Seafaring* 1971

J. H. Betts 'Ships on Minoan Seals' *Colston Papers* (1973)

Chr. Blinkenberg 'Triemiolia etc' Arch.-Kunsthist.-Medd. det Kgl. Danske Videnskabernes Selskab II 3 (1938)

L. Casson 'the Supergalleys etc' *MM* 55 (1969) = Casson (1969); *Ships and Seamanship in the Ancient World* 1971

J. A. Davison 'The first Triremes' *Class. Quart.* 41 (1947)

H. Frost 'Punic Ship' *IJNA* ii l, iii 1, *MM* 60 3 (1973-4)

M. I. Finley *Early Greece* 1970

B. Landström *The Ships of the Pharaohs* 1970

A. B. Lloyd 'Triremes in the Saite Navy' *JEA* 58 (1972)

J. S. Morrison, R. T. Williams *Greek Oared Ships* 1966 *GOS*; J. S. Morrison 'The first Triremes' *MM* 65 i (1979); 'Hemiolia, Trihemiolia' *IJNA* 8 3 (1979)

W. L. Rodgers *Naval Warfare Under Oars* 1940

J. Rougé *La marine dans l'antiquité* 1975

N. K. Sandars *The Sea Peoples* 1979

C. G. Starr '*The Roman Imperial Navy*' *31* BC-AD *324* 1960

H. W. Swiny, M. L. Katzev 'The Kyrenia Shipwreck' *CP* (1973)

W. W. Tarn 'The Dedicated Ship etc' *JHS* 30 (1910) = Tarn (1910); *Hellenistic Military and Naval Developments* 1930

A. Tchernia, P. Pomey, A. Hesnard 'L'épave romaine de la Madrague de Giens' xxxive supplément à *Gallia* (1979)

The Bronze Age: 3000–1200 BC

A survey of Bronze Age ships in the Mediterranean provides a useful introduction to an account of the various types of ships employed in that area in the civilizations of Greece and Rome.

Representations and models of Egyptian river craft survive from very early times, and in the Cheops ship (*ca.*2650 BC) a complete wooden hull is extant, 43.4m long and 5.9m broad, flat-bottomed and without a keel. During the 5th dynasty of the Old Kingdom (*ca.*2560–*ca.*2420 BC) sea-going ships, returning from a voyage to Byblos on the Levant coast, are shown in relief in the temple of King Sahure at Abusir near Cairo. In the records 'Byblos ships' is a general term for sea-going ships, so it may be concluded that the coastal run to Byblos was the regular, but not necessarily the only, sea-route from the Nile Delta. The cities of the Levant and Syria could supply the metals and timber which Egypt lacked. Voyages to Punt, probably on the coast of Somalia, are also mentioned for the import of myrrh, electrum and ebony, and to Sinai for turquoise. The ships shown in this relief have a gently rising bow and stern, a mast of twin poles and a massive rope truss passing fore and aft raised on supports and holding the bow and stern overhang in tension by means of a spar passed through the rope amidships, twisted and made fast. The purpose of the truss is apparently to prevent the probably keelless hull from breaking its back in a seaway. No sails are shown since the mast has been lowered and lies on a massive support (or crutch).

Plate 1 Relief at Medinet Habu in Egypt. About 1176 BC. After *Journal of Near Eastern Studies* 2 (1943), 40, fig.4. By courtesy of the Chicago University Press.

Plate 2 (*a*) Lead model of a long ship from Naxos. The gently rising end is the stern. The forefoot has been bent upwards. Before 2500 BC. Photo: Ashmolean Museum, Oxford. (*b*) Fan-shaped terracotta from Syros depicting a ship. The stern rises more sharply than in (*a*). There is a projecting forefoot. Sixteen oars are indicated on each side. After 2500 BC. In the National Museum at Athens. (*c*) Drawing of a ship of a Northwest Anatolian type on a dagger from Dorak. After 2500 BC. After J.Mellaart, *The Chalcolithic and Early Bronze Ages in the Near East and Anatolia* (1966), fig.53, p.170.

With these Egyptian cargo-carriers may be contrasted the long, narrow, oared craft of about the same period which are represented by the Naxos lead models, on the Syros 'fans', and in more detail and under sail on the silver dagger from Dorak in North-West Anatolia (Pl.2 a, b, and c.). These Aegean ships show in the bow a projecting forefoot which is characteristic throughout antiquity of one type of Mediterranean hull, the galley, or long ship (as both Greeks and Romans called it), in distinction from the round ships or caiques. In the later battle fleets this forefoot is metal-sheathed and used as a ram, but at this stage it seems to have been a structural feature, the continuation of the keel forward beyond the stempost rather than a deliberately contrived ram (see p.55, below).

In Crete in the 3rd millennium, ships of both types, asymmetrical with forefoot, and symmetrical with rising bow and stern, are represented on seals (see Casson (1971) pl.34–45 and J.H.Betts (1973)). The Cretans in the 16th century traded as far west as Apulia, Sicily and the Lipari Islands, and with Libya. They seem to have spread their outposts also over the eastern Mediterranean, and Cretan traders are said in the Homeric *Hymn to Apollo* to have been the first priests of Apollo at Delphi. Since archaeology attests both the wealth of the Cretan palaces of this period and also their lack of fortification, historians have been inclined to accept, in spite of the lack of evidence for Cretan warships, Thucydides' attribution of naval supremacy to Crete. But more recently the freedom of the seas from war-fleets has been attributed rather to the balance of land power between Egypt and the Hittite empire.

In Egypt Queen Hatshepsut's grave-temple relief of the 16th/15th century shows oared merchant vessels with rising bow and stern, twin rudder oars, fifteen oarsmen a side, masts of single poles and sails elaborately rigged with yardarm and boom. There is a thick fore-and-aft rope truss with a device for making taut. The inscription shows that the ships are returning, presumably to a Red Sea port, from Punt, and the cargo, which because of the occupation of the lower part of the hull by oarsmen is necessarily on deck, visibly consists of jars and casks and shrub-like trees in pots. These ships are the first examples of a type which recurs throughout antiquity (see Pl.37 p.53 below), the merchantman which has a single row of oars on each side and hence carries its cargo on deck.

Belonging to about the same period, the 15th century BC, is the recently discovered miniature fresco on the walls of a room in the Western House at Akrotiri, Thera (modern Santorini) (Pl. 4), which shows a large number of ships and boats moving from left to right along a coastline, from a river delta with palm-trees and animals to a city harbour. The ships, of sickle shape with gently rising bow and stern, are painted in vivid colours and gaily decorated; and the fresco radiates an atmosphere of happy activity and enjoyment, the energy of the paddlers and the sponge-divers contrasting with the relaxation of the passengers. The larger ships are paddled with sails lowered but the mast up, although there is a crutch on which it could be lowered. These ships are apparently just coming into harbour. In the best-preserved of them there are 21 paddlers shown on the starboard side, an important person in a canopied cabin in the stern, and nine other people under a large canopy amidships, above which is a (square) sail, lowered and furled, with yardarm and boom resting on the canopy.

Plate 3 Egyptian sea-going ships depicted on a relief in the temple of Queen Hatshepsut at Deir-el-Bahari. About 1500BC. After A.Mariette, *Deir-el-Bahari* (1877), pl.6.

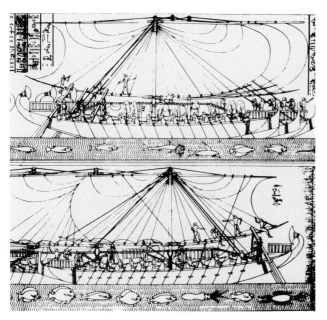

In one case the mast is up, in two cases the mast, like the yardarm and boom, rests on the canopy, or rather on its supports. The paddlers appear to sit in an open gallery on each side of the canopied area, so that the ship must have been quite broad. A remarkable, and unparalleled, feature of the larger ships is what appears to be a permanently fixed boarding plank on both sides of the stern. The feature is perhaps less surprising when it is remembered that later long and round ships (see below Pl.15 p. 19) visibly carried ladders for stern boarding. A permanently fixed boarding plank would be a suitable convenience for a large passenger vessel. The smaller vessels on the fresco do not have it, because a man could easily step from the ground on to the projecting ends of the stern crossbeam (see *GOS*

p. 54). One of the smaller ships is being rowed with the mast and sail up, a procedure of which Homer would not have approved. The rigging is simple: four lifts on the port and four on the starboard side, in each case two attached to the yard and two to the boom. There are also four braces from the yard which come back to the steersman and enable him to control its set. If these ships are, as they appear to be, passenger vessels or light cargo-carriers, the paddles would have been employed only for entering and leaving port, but are nevertheless remarkable in sea-going vessels of this degree of sophistication. Paddles had given place to oars in Egyptian river craft by about 2400 BC. It is uncertain where the scene depicted on the fresco is to be placed geographically, and hence how the ships and people are to be identified. As the ships differ from contemporary Egyptian craft, so are they to be contrasted with the Syrian merchantmen depicted on an Egyptian relief (now destroyed) in the tomb of

Plate 4 Detail of a fresco in the Western House at Akrotiri, Thera (mod. Santorini). 1500–1400 BC. In National Museum, Athens.

Kenamun of *ca.*1400 BC. These show a symmetrical hull with vertical stem and stern posts, rising more steeply at bow and stern than the Akrotiri ships. They are tubbier craft, proceeding under sail, and clearly designed for cargo-carrying. The 9m cargo ship wrecked towards the end of the 13th century BC off Cape Gelidonya in south-west Turkey is likely to have been of this type, though little of its hull remains. Its cargo was a collection of ingots of copper, bronze and tin, a metal-worker's tools and merchant's weights as well a miscellaneous collection of scrap metal.

Cyprus seems to have been the entrepôt between the Levant and the Mycenaean world. In the 13th century the Mycenaeans had outposts at Miletus and on the Anatolian coast at Colophon and Tarsus. The Homeric poems look back to the period of Mycenaean power and expansion. But it is to be noted that although they have as their theme a Mycenaean sea-borne expedition

Plate 5 Ships represented on the tomb of Kenamun. About 1400 BC After *Journal of Egyptian Archaeology* 33 (1947), pl.8. By courtesy of the Egypt Exploration Society.

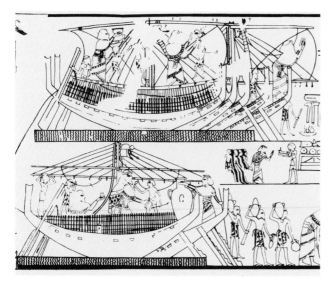

and its aftermath, there are no sea-battles, since Troy, rather surprisingly in view of her geographical position, has no fleet. In the *Odyssey* there are plenty of pirate-traders, mostly Phoenician, on the high seas. The concept of thalassocracy, domination of the seas by a powerful fleet, seems to be quite absent. A naval expedition is the transport of fighting men to a place where they will fight on land. We may give up the siege of Troy as an historical event, but naval expeditions of that kind are likely to have been typical of the age. The Trojan war may have been, as N.K.Sandars has well put it, 'a paradigm of many sieges, many quarrels, many flights and many returns' in the memory of the Greeks of the 8th century. But the Catalogue of Ships in the second book of the *Iliad* is probably something different. It records in terms of contingents of ships assembled for the expedition against Troy the relative power of the different parts of the Mycenaean world in the period of its greatness. The ships are oared galleys, and in one squadron of seven ships (*Il.* II 719–720) 'fifty oarsmen sat in each ship', i.e. the ships were what were later called pentecontors (50-oar ships). In each of the Boeotians' 50 ships 'went a hundred and twenty young men of the Boeotians' (*Il.* II 509–10), but the poet does not say that they all rowed, though Thucydides, commenting on the Catalogue, says that they did. By the 8th century, when the *Iliad* was being put together, two levels of oars on each side were being introduced. A ship of 60 oars a side at two levels is not an impossibility for the 8th century but is most unlikely earlier. The ships of Odysseus in the *Odyssey* are pentecontors with 50 oarsmen and two officers in each. We may think of the Mycenaean ships as descending directly from the ships of the Syros 'fans', from those modelled in lead on Naxos and those etched on the sword from Dorak (see above Pl.2).

At the end of the 13th or the beginning of the 12th century the Mycenaean world began to collapse, either from internal or from external causes, or from a combination of both. Pylos, unlike Mycenae and Tiryns, was unfortified, and the invasion, or attack, which destroyed her came at least partly by sea. The fire of her destruction baked and preserved the clay tablets which refer to rowers, one to about 30 men from five towns sent to Pleuron, possibly the Pleuron in Aetolia, another to 570 + rowers, i.e. crew for 19 ships if they were triacontors, 11 ships if they were pentecontors. These appear to be dispositions to meet the attack. A galley depicted on a clay box in the Pylos-Tragana tomb in Messenia and dated 1200–1100 BC may be envisaged as the sort of ship the defenders of Pylos used (Pl.6). There is a surprising amount of detail: a high-rising stern with fenced steersman's seat, rudder oar and rudder-oar handle (or tiller), a similarly high fenced f'c'sle with the stempost stepped vertically into the keel which projects forward beyond it. We may accept provisionally the explanation that the uprights surmounted by a horizontal line represent the rowing benches and the far gunwale. There is a forestay, and two backstays running from the top of the mast aft. The lowest of the three ropes running aft is likely to have been attached to the end of the yardarm and thus to have been a brace, and is so restored. There is a single sail.

The age which saw the collapse of the Mycenaean civilization and end of the Hittite empire also witnessed the movement of peoples down from Syria through Palestine to the Delta. They came by land with their oxcarts and families, and also by sea. Their repulse is celebrated in a magnificent monument erected by Rameses III at Medinet Habu, which contains a picture in relief of the sea-battle (Pl.1). There are four Egyptian oared ships shown with between six and eleven oarsmen a side, the mast and the yardarm are up and the sail furled. On each ship there are bowmen, not on a deck but standing between the oarsmen. These ships, of quite a modest rating, are apparently driving five ships of the enemy, one of

Plate 6 Long ship on a clay box from the Pylos-Tragana tomb. 1200–1100 BC. After *GOS*, pl.1.

which has capsized, towards the shore, where more Egyptian bowmen are drawn up in front of a huge figure of the Pharaoh Rameses. The Egyptian ships are sickle-shaped with high stern- and lower bow-'castles', crow's nests and side-screens, while the ships of the invaders, closely resembling the Syrian ships of the Kenamun tomb (see Pl.5 p.12 above) have symmetrical bow and stern posts but in other respects resemble the Egyptian ships. They have no oars, but like the Egyptian ships have mast and yardarm raised with sail furled. N.K.Sandars has said that they must have had oars to have reached the Delta, although none are shown. But it is inconceivable that if they had had oars they would not have used them in battle where they would be most useful. It looks as if Rameses' fleet of small ships carrying bowmen had succeeded in catching at sea and driving ashore a squadron of sailing ships accompanying the invaders, which might have aimed at landing and capturing a strongpoint in the path of their land force. The Harris papyrus written after the death of Rameses III in 1162 speaks of cargo-ships, equipped with bowmen and soldiers, built for the trade with Syria and 'the countries at the ends of the earth'. It seems that in Egypt, and probably elsewhere in the Levant, there was hardly a distinction at this time between warships and cargo-ships.

Long Ships of the Archaic Age

It has been said that the Dark Age which followed the collapse of the Mycenaean civilization in Greece is a dark age only in the sense that we know very little about it. The same might be said very aptly about the maritime history of the 11th, 10th and 9th centuries in the Mediterranean. Men must have continued to use the sea highways for their lawful and unlawful occasions, in long oared galleys and in round cargo ships, but there are almost no monuments to represent their ships and no records of their voyages.

However, in the 8th century three developments took place. The first of these is shown by a series of grave vases in the Late Geometric style which begin to

Plate 7
(*a*) (below) Fragments of an Attic krater Louvre A 527. 760–735 BC.

(*b*) (right) Fragments of an Attic krater Louvre A 527. 760–735 BC.

Photos: Musée du Louvre, Paris.

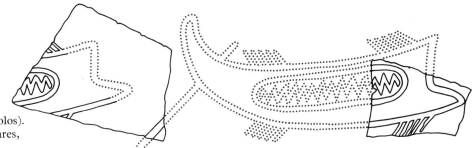

Plate 8 Fragments of a Middle Helladic vase from Iolkos (mod. Volos). About 1600 BC. After D.R.Theochares, *Archaeology* (1958), 15.

show, among the regular ornament of scenes of funerals, chariot processions and land battles, also scenes of fighting from ships which appear to be beached (7a and b). The ships then are still transports for fighting men, not yet themselves weapons of war. These scenes serve to illustrate for us the ships described in the Homeric poems in such detail, since they derive from the time at which it is thought that these poems were composed. The interpretation of Geometric ship pictures is not easy. The Pylos ship (Pl.6) shows bow and stern platforms joined at the base by a horizontal line from which a series of vertical lines descend to the hull. Comparison with another Bronze Age representation (Pl.8) which seems to combine a bird's eye view with a side view of a ship suggests that this horizontal line joining the bow and stern platforms must be taken for the top of the far side of the ship (i.e. the far gunwale), and the verticals for the oarsmen's benches. A similar conventional treatment of perspective seems to be shown on the Geometric vases. The thick horizontal line joining bow and stern platforms and the verticals which are seen below and crossing it must be taken for the far gunwale with its rail and for the rowing benches, respectively. Both gunwales have a rail, and in some pictures 'fish-hook'-shaped rowlocks are also seen. The height of the ship above the waterline has been unrealistically increased to produce the perspective required, but if the

necessary correction is made these vessels would appear as the same light craft as Theseus' 30-oared ship portrayed with more realistic perspective on the François vase in Florence from the first half of the sixth century (Pl.9). In the Geometric ships the artist makes no attempt to show all the oarsmen, and the human figures shown either at the oars or steering or elsewhere are, by an artistic convention consistent throughout antiquity, grossly out of scale with the ship. On the François vase the figures though out of scale are not grossly so, and it does accordingly give a much better impression than most of what an ancient ship, in this case an open, undecked, triacontor, must have looked like.

The Aristonothos vase (Pl.10), made probably in Italy in the first half of the 7th century, shows an interesting encounter between two ships of distinct

Plate 9 Drawing of a long ship from an Attic black-figure volute krater by Kleitias. About 600–550 BC. Florence 4209 (the François vase).

types. The ship on the left is a long ship of what can be called the Aegean type, with high stern, low bow, six oarports and five out-of-scale oarsmen, and what appears to be a fore-and-aft gangway or narrow deck connecting the bow and stern platforms. On this gangway three out-of-scale soldiers in armour are standing. The exaggerated size of the oarsmen and soldiers is responsible for their small numbers. The exaggerated size of the soldiers is also responsible for the invention of the gangway or deck, since they would normally stand on the bow platform in attacking another ship. This would appear to be a real sea-fight with the forefoot of the long ship now used offensively as a ram. This development is confirmed by the ship to the right of the picture which appears to be a symmetrically hulled ship in which a ram has been built on to an upcurving bow. The resultant shape is recognizable Etruscan. The feature seems to indicate that ramming was now an obligatory naval tactic and that hulls without a natural ram had to be adapted to

take one. The picture may record a clash between Greeks and Etruscans in the period of Greek intrusion into Italian waters.

In the latter part of the 6th century there is a number of Attic vases showing galleys at sea under oar and sail. They decorate the inner rim of wine vessels (*dinoi*) and would have appeared to ride on the wine when the *dinos* was full. In these the steersman and the heads of the oarsmen are visible. The long ship shown in Pl.11 is rowed by 25 oarsmen on the port side, and thus appears as a 50-oared ship, i.e., a pentecontor. But below the v-shaped rowlocks in the gunwale through which the oars are being rowed there is what appears to be a row of 25 oarports. If these really are oarports, the ship must be potentially a ship of 50 oars a side, like the Boeotian ships in the Homeric Catalogue (see p.12 above) or the regular dromons as described by Leo VI (see p.50 below) in the 9th century AD. Another *dinos* (Pl.12) shows a one-level triacontor. Together with a 6th century relief of a longship without oars, oarsmen or rigging (the Basel relief), the *dinos* ships give a very vivid idea of the earlier long-ships of 30 and 50 oars, the triacontors and pentecontors. These were the ships in which the

Plate 10 (*a*) and (*b*) Two ships of different types on a krater probably West Greek by Aristonothos in the Palazzo dei Conservatori, Rome. 700–650 BC. Photo: Vasari.

Plate 11 Long ship on the inner rim of an Attic black-figure *dinos* by Exekias. 550–530 BC. Villa Giulia Museum, Rome, 50599. Photo: Vasari.

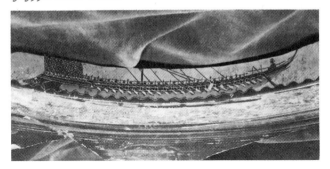

Plate 12 Long ship on the inner rim of an Attic black-figure *dinos* by the Antimenes painter. About 530–510 BC. Madrid, 1092. Photo: Museo Arqeológico, Madrid.

colonizing voyages were made in the 8th, 7th, and 6th centuries from mainland Greece, the Aegean islands and the coast of Asia Minor to Africa, to the west as far as Massilia (modern Marseille) and to the coasts of the Black Sea. Cyrene is said to have been founded from Thera (Santorini) by a colonizing party in two pentecontors. In 543 BC when the Persian attack on the Ionian Greeks was imminent the Phocaeans embarked their families and possessions in pentecontors and sailed into the western Mediterranean (Herodotus I 164[3]). These pentecontors are likely to have been the same ships as those in which five years later they

engaged a combined fleet of Carthaginians and Etruscans off Sardinia at Alalia, and as Herodotus says (I 166[12]) won a dubious victory with 60 ships lost and the remaining 20 useless because 'they had had their rams twisted off'. It appears then that by the second half of the 6th century at least the projection of the keel forward, the forefoot, had been armoured for use offensively in a sea-battle between ships as units. It was this metal sheath which was twisted off at Alalia. The age of the warship as such, rather than as a transport for fighting men, had arrived.

The second new development affected oar-power. Towards the end of the 8th and the beginning of the 7th century there are certain indications that the naval tactic of the ram had introduced pressure for greater power and manoeuvrability in the oared warship. The increase from 15 men a side in the triacontor to 25 men a side in the pentecontor, with a corresponding increase of more than nine metres in length and some increase also in breadth, was probably made as much in the interests of carrying men and gear as to produce a more powerful and efficient warship. But the introduction of ramming tactics would underline the need for a good ratio of oarsmen to length and for ways to use the maximum oar-power with minimum overall weight. The first step in this direction seems to have been taken towards the end of the 8th century. The Boeotian ships in the Homeric Catalogue may have been rowed by 120 oarsmen at two levels and an Attic spouted bowl dated 735–710 BC (Pl.13) may depict 39 oarsmen at two levels on the starboard side of a long-ship. Alternatively, the upper row of 19 oarsmen may be the port side file shown in primitive perspective. But the two-level system is illustrated unequivocally on the reliefs from the palace of Sennacherib at Nineveh which record the evacuation of Tyre by sea (Pl.14a and b). The ships are of two types, the Aegean with up-curving stern and ram-bow and the symmetrical Syrian or Phoenician type. Both

Plate 13 Long ship possibly with oars at two levels on an Attic spouted bowl. About 735–710 BC. London, XCII B 64. Photo: reproduced by courtesy of the Trustees of the British Museum.

Plate 14 (a) Fragment of a relief from the palace of Sennacherib at Nineveh depicting long and round ships. 701 BC. Photo: reproduced by courtesy of the Trustees of the British Museum. (b) Another relief from the same source. Photograph kindly supplied by the Director, Department of West Asian Antiquities, British Museum.

are rowed by two levels of oarsmen on each side, the upper sitting above and between the lower file. The date of this event is 701 BC. The historian Damastes of Sigeum, writing in Asia Minor in the late 5th century BC, says (Jacoby FGrH 5 F6) that the invention of two-level ships was made by the Erythraeans in Ionia, but he gives no indication of date. The invention may have been Phoenician, since we see it first definitely at Tyre, but the mixture of Aegean and Syrian types of ship in the evacuation fleet indicates that Levantine shipping at this date was coming under Greek influence, which suggests that two levels of oars as well as the ram-bow may have been a borrowing from the Greeks of Ionia. A fragment of a proto-Attic vase from Phalerum (*GOS* pl.8a) of 700–650 BC also shows unmistakably that the two-level system was being employed in mainland Greece at about this time. At the end of the 6th century a fine Attic black-figure cup shows two pentecontors both rowed at two levels, although in one some of the upper file of oars are not manned (Pl.15a and b).

The third development led to the invention of the trireme. The first step was the evolution of the oared

warship as an offensive weapon by arming the forefoot as a ram. The introduction of the second level of oarsmen towards the latter part of the 8th century appears to have been the second step. The third step seem to have been taken almost immediately. Vitruvius (I 24) called the distance between one rowlock of a file of oarsmen and the next on the gunwale the *interscalmium* and gives the length as 2 cubits (0.888 m). To this basic unit of an oared galley there were two men in a two-level ship. The next step increased the number to three. Looking at the matter from a different view-point, one can say that in a single level ship there is one file of oarsmen on each side, 15 oarsmen a side in a triacontor and 25 in a pentecontor. In a two-level ship there are two files on each side of the ship. By the next step there were three.

Thucydides (I 13), writing of the early history of Greece at the end of the 5th century, says that increased power and wealth led to tyrannies and naval armament: 'And the Corinthians are said to have applied themselves to naval affairs in a manner very close to the modern and triremes are said to have been built in Corinth for the first time in Greece. It appears that Ameinocles, a Corinthian shipwright, built four ships for the Samians also; and it was about 300 years before the end of the Peloponnesian war that Ameinocles visited the Samians. And the most ancient sea-battle we know was between the Corinthians and the Corcyraeans; and this was 270 years before the same date.' 'The end of this war' could be either 404 BC, when the Peloponnesian war, the theme of Thucydides' history, ended, or 421 BC when the early part of it, the Archidamian war, came to an end, depending on the date at which Thucydides wrote the passage. The former is the more probable. The date of Ameinocles' visit to Samos would then be 704 BC, unless, as has been suggested, in converting into years a system of reckoning backwards by generations Thucydides has wrongly used a generation of 40 years

instead of the rule of thumb used by his predecessor Herodotus by which three generations are equated with 100 years. If this suggestion is right, the date of Ameinocles' visit must be lowered by 50 years. There are thus uncertainties about the exact date intended but these uncertainties do not affect the main fact to

Plate 15 (*a*) and (*b*) Two long ships with two levels of oars and two round ships shown on a black-figure cup in the British Museum. 550–500 BC. Photo: reproduced by courtesy of the Trustees of the British Museum.

which Thucydides testifies, that Ameinocles at some time after the invention of the trireme at Corinth built some for the Samians too. Whether this happened at the end of the end of the 8th or in the middle of the 7th century is not of great importance.

The invention of the trireme at Corinth is likely to have been the result of the pressure of naval competition, and it is hard not to take this as the thought which links together Thucydides' statement about the building of triremes at Corinth and his further remark that the first sea-battle took place between the Corinthians and the Corcyraeans 30 years later. And it need not be concluded that the naval competition which led to the building of the trireme was necessarily in the first instance the result of competition between Corinth and Corcyra. It is more likely to have been confrontation at sea between Corinth and the pirates, Etruscans and others, against whom Corinth would have had to establish her trading position in the Adriatic. As Thucydides goes on to say: 'Corinth acquired ships', i.e. triremes, 'put down piracy...'. Corcyra was founded by Corinth in 720 BC and her position commanding the entrance to the Corinthian Gulf seems to have led her into conflict with her mother city. The naval competition, leading to the invention of the trireme, and the sea-battle, could have taken place before the establishment of the tyranny at Corinth (*ca.* 650 BC). Indeed had the first building of triremes taken place there during the tyranny it is difficult to believe that it would not have been associated with the name of the tyrant Periander. But this is not the case. It has been argued that the first sentence of the passage of Thucydides above, which gives the results of the increasing power and prosperity of Greece as (i) the establishment of tyrannies (about 650 BC) and (ii) the fitting out of navies and greater reliance on the sea, is inconsistent with a statement which apparently places the building of the first triremes at Corinth several decades before the establishment of the tyranny there. But Thucydides' first sentence is a very general one and can hardly be taken to imply a close chronological connection between the establishment of tyrannies and the fitting out of navies.

Granted that what Thucydides is saying is that triremes were first built in Greece at Corinth towards the end of the 8th century (or 50 years later), it has been argued that the account is so improbable that it must be rejected. It is improbable because 'the clumsy and unseaworthy triremes of Salamis' were by that account the products of 220 years of evolution, 'though little over ten years more were needed for the revolutionary changes in construction, manning and tactics which gave the Athenians nearly sixty years of almost unchallengeable supremacy at sea'. This picture will be shown to be erroneous. The triremes of Salamis were neither more clumsy nor more unseaworthy than the triremes of the Peloponnesian war; and such changes as there were followed a temporary shift in the conception of the proper role of the trireme in battle. The point of substance which must be explained is the long and slow progress of the trireme from its first use in Corinth to its position as a ship of the line in all the navies of the 5th century. But Thucydides is in fact at pains to account for this slow development in the passage which immediately follows the text quoted. 'The Corinthians', he says, 'acquired ships' (again, in the context, certainly triremes) 'suppressed piracy and became rich in their position on the isthmus where they could command the transit trade by land and sea'. In this period is to be placed Periander's connection with the Egyptian Pharaoh Necho and the latter's consequent construction of triremes, as Herodotus related, and use of them in the Red Sea, probably for the suppression of piracy. There is no reason to believe that these were a special type evolved independently in Phoenicia. The main piece of evidence on which this latter theory rests is the Erment clay model (Pl.34) of a three-level ship deriving from the end of the 4th or the beginning of the 3rd century. I shall argue that this model represents one of the large three-level polyremes which were being developed at that time (see below p.42) Thucydides next refers to the Ionian Greeks who 'had large navies in the time of Cyrus and his son Cambyses' (549–522 BC), then to Polycrates, tyrant of Samos, and to the Phocaeans who 'in the process of planting the colony of Massilia defeated the Carthaginians in a sea-battle'. To this period belongs a fragment of the Ionian poet Hipponax (frg.45 Diehl: *GOS* p.120), which contains the first literary mention of a trireme, and incidentally refers to its ram. Thucydides then sums up the whole account of sea-power from Corinth onwards as follows: 'These were the most powerful of the fleets. It appears that even these... employed few triremes, but still were equipped like the Trojan war fleets with pentecontors and long ships'. This last sentence has been taken to refer only to the fleets of Massilia and Carthage, but the run of the passage as well as the reference to the Trojan war fleets indicates that it is a statement about Greek fleets in general. As such it is a most important pronouncement and shows Thucydides' awareness that the slow and gradual introduction of the trireme as the ship of the line was something which needed explanation.

The final paragraph of Thucydides' survey runs as follows: 'Shortly before the Persian wars and the death of Darius' (486 BC) 'triremes in large numbers were at the disposal of the tyrants in Sicily and of the Corcyraeans. These were the last of the fleets of note in Greece to be established before the expedition of Xerxes. For the Aeginetans and the Athenians and some others had acquired small fleets, and most of these were pentecontors. It was late in the day that Themistocles persuaded the Athenians who were at war with the Aeginetans, and when the barbarian was expected, to construct the ships with which they fought at Salamis. And these did not yet have decks right across'.

In conclusion, although there were undoubtedly omissions in Thucydides' very general account of the growth of Greek sea-power and of the part played in it by the trireme, there is nothing improbable about it. The trireme appears to have been an expensive naval weapon built for a specific purpose and requiring high standards of training and skill. Only the most successful and ambitious states afforded it, and they only when faced with the need to suppress piracy or the prospect of naval confrontation. Invented probably in the context of naval competition, it is not surprising that it was not used on a big scale until the increasing prosperity of mainland Greece and the major power clashes of the 5th century produced the fleets of triremes in their hundreds of the Persian wars and of Athens in the exercise of a naval hegemony in the Aegean.

As support for the argument that 'the first introduction of the trireme into Greek navies should be dated in the third quarter of the sixth century and preferably nearer to 525 than 550' it has been observed that 'there are no signs of anything which anyone has tried to identify as a trireme on any vase plaque or relief of the sixth century or earlier, though the fragment of Hipponax suggests that this is an accident and that Ionian artists were portraying triremes towards the end of the sixth century'. The truth is that very few representations of ships of any kind have survived from the places where triremes were employed in the early period, i.e. Corinth, Ionia, and western Greece. The representations virtually all come from Athens which had very few if any triremes in her fleets before the 5th century. The lack of representations is therefore accidental not only for the 6th century but for the 7th and 8th as well, and proves nothing about the date of the first introduction of the trireme into Greek fleets.

The Age of the Trireme

In 482 BC Themistocles proposed, and the Athenians agreed, to spend the surplus deriving from the silver mines at Laurium, not on a share-out to all qualified citizens, as the Thasians in similar circumstances had done, but on building a fleet of 200 triremes, which not only gave her naval superiority over her immediate neighbour, with whom she was at war, but also put her on competitive terms with the naval powers of the Eastern Mediterranean and the West. The Persians had launched a sea-borne attack on Attica in 490 and had been defeated as they came ashore in the Bay of Marathon. It was expected that they would come again; and Themistocles' proposal showed a clear intention of meeting at sea the immensely greater forces which Persia could deploy from the Greek cities of Asia Minor, from Phoenicia and from Egypt. The slow introduction of the trireme in large numbers into mainland Greek fleets up to now had been due in part to lack of challenge and in part to lack of resources. Athens now had both. The trireme was, as a recent writer has said, 'vulnerable, unseaworthy, and ludicrously expensive to man and maintain', but a fleet of triremes was the subscription rate for the big-power league; and ambitious states, first Corinth in the days of her prosperity, then the tyrants, in the east Polycrates who added 40 triremes to a fleet of 100 pentecontors, and in the west Hiero and Gelon, and lastly Athens, were ready and able to pay it. Vulnerable and unseaworthy it might be, but in the chosen conditions of battle and manned by experts it was the most efficient fighting machine yet devised. It was fortunate

Plate 16 (*a*) and (*b*) Model of a two-level oared ship based on the long ships in pl.15 (a) and (b).

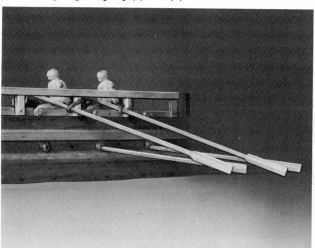
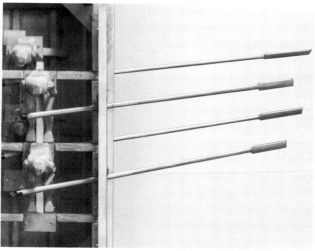

for the Greek world of the 5th century that there were states who could afford the subscription and thus were in a position to repel the powers which threatened it by sea, Carthage from the west and Persia with her maritime allies from the east.

The literary and archaeological evidence for the trireme in the 5th and 4th centuries does not amount to much. It is by no means commensurate with the role it played in the history of the time. But we can be fairly confident that we know the main facts about it. The evidence is set out in some detail in *GOS*; here it may be summarized. The first step taken to improve the length/oar-power ratio of the long ship was a comparatively easy one. The oar-power was doubled (or the length halved) by setting a second file of oarsmen on each side of the ship above and between the original file (see model Pl.16). The next step produced the trireme. We must now ask the question what this step was. The first fact which must influence the answer is that a passage in Thucydides (II 93) shows

without doubt that a trireme was rowed by oarsmen working single-manned oars, so that an explanation of a trireme sitting two or three men to an oar is ruled out. The second fact is attested in another passage of Thucydides. It appears from VII 34[5] that the trireme had beams projecting on each side of the bow (Gr. *epotides*: 'things like ears') and that these were forward of and protected something called in Greek *parexeiresia* i.e. 'beside-out-rowing', in other words, a structure built out from the ship's side to accommodate the rowlocks of oarsmen sitting too close to the gunwale to be able to have their rowlocks on it. In a modern racing eight, the structure is called an outrigger. This feature may be regarded as the development which made a ship of three files, or oarsmen, a side possible if the oars were single-manned. And it is easy to see why. If three files are to row on each side of the ship, each man working one oar, the optimum arrangement, i.e. the one by which all the oars in one unit or *interscalmium* (see above p.19) are of the same length (the length suited to an average man's strength), is when the added third file of oarsmen is placed immediately above the lowest but further

Plate 17 (*a*) and (*b*) Model of a three-level oared ship based on the Lenormant relief (pl.20) and the Talos vase (pl.19).

Plate 18 Fragment of an Attic red-figure cup in Vienna University Museum, 503.48. About 450 BC. Photograph by courtesy of the University of Vienna.

Plate 19 Attic red-figure volute krater by the Talos painter. Jatta Collection, Ruvo, Italy. After Furtwängler-Reichold.

outboard, and accordingly worked his oar through an outrigger. The model shown in Pl. 17 is the same model as appeared in Pl. 16, but a third file and an outrigger have been added in the way described. Three representations of ships survive from Athens in the 5th century, showing three rowing levels. A 4th type appears on *bullae* (seals) from Persepolis and dates from some time between 520/13 and 331 BC (Pl. 17). This last shows three levels of oars, but the impression is much worn and it is impossible to say whether an outrigger is shown or not. A small fragment (Pl. 18) of a red-figure vase, now in Vienna, shows three pairs of horizontal wales on the (probably starboard) side of a long ship. Between the lowest pair there is one oarport, between the middle pair two oarports and between the uppermost pair (which probably represent an open rail) none. Above are two in-curving stanchions which support a narrow deck with a rail. Vertical lines pass through the deck (? mast and tackle) and above is what appears to be the bunched bottom corner of the sail (the 'foot').

The second representation is on an Attic krater by the Talos painter in the Ruvo museum (Pl. 19) and consists of the stern and part of the hull of the Argo, which is beached. The artist has shown, by a fortunate anachronism, the port side of a trireme. At the lowest level between wales is an oarport, on which the artist has attempted to draw the leather bag (gr. *askoma*) which was fitted at this level to prevent the entry of water in rough weather. At a higher level are three oarports and above them a double rail in which rowlocks are shown. This double rail is supported by pairs of stays at intervals. In each pair one is curved and rests on the upper wale and the other is straight and rests on the lower wale. The fact that the latter slopes outwards in front of the upper row of oarports indicates that the upper rail equipped with rowlocks is in fact an outrigger. Above it is a broad deck supported by stanchions which curve outwards. The size of the figures is, as usual, greatly out of proportion to the ship.

It seems that the artist of the Ruvo painting gives in much more detail a ship which is basically similar to the ship shown on the Vienna fragment, except that the deck-stanchions curve the other way, showing that the former has a broad and the latter a narrow deck. In the latter there are no stays supporting the uppermost pair of horizontal planks, yet since this pair shows no portholes it seems likely that it represents an outrigger and that the artist has omitted the stays. The fact that the Ruvo ship's upper portholes continue further into the stern than the lower is likely to be the result of the contraction of the hull in the stern.

The third and most informative of the 5th century representations is the Lenormant relief (Pl.20), which shows nearly a third of the starboard rowing compartment (nine out of the 31 uppermost (thranite)) oarsmen. The oarsmen, here necessarily in scale with the ship, row through an outrigger supported, like the outrigger in the Talos vase ship, by pairs of stays. The oars of the middle-level oarsmen (zygian), who are invisible, emerge from underneath the outrigger and the oars of the lowest level (thalamian), also invisible, emerge from oarports apparently fitted with the *askoma*. The deck over the heads of the thranite oarsmen is supported as in the Talos vase ship by outward curving stanchions, showing that the relief like the vase but unlike the Vienna fragment depicts a wide-decked ship.

Finally, there are the Persepolis *bullae* (seals) which are dated either in the last quarter of the 5th or in the first three quarters of the 4th century. They show ships, probably Phoenician, with three levels of oars. The surface is too damaged to make out an outrigger and three-dimensional features must in any case be doubtful, but in one impression several pairs of stays are seen rising from a wale to where the outrigger would be. The ships are then to be regarded as triremes of the normal kind.

The remaining important items of evidence from the 5th and 4th centuries relating to the trireme may be listed as follows:

(i) the maximum dimensions of the Piraeus ship-sheds which were built in the 5th century and rebuilt on the same foundations after their destruction in 404 BC (*GOS* Blackman p.181) are 35 m by 4.8 m. Triremes could not have been any longer or broader than this.

(ii) the number of men in the ship's company attested consistently from the 6th to the 4th century (*GOS* p.129 and 254) is 200.

(iii) the length of the oars is given in the lists of naval equipment in the Athenian dockyards at Piraeus preserved for a few years from the second quarter of the 4th century (*GOS* p.289) as 9 and 9½ cubits (4 m or 4.2 m). It is likely that the shorter oars are used, as in a modern naval cutter, in the positions towards the bow and stern where the hull contracts.

(iv) the dockyard lists also provide evidence (*GOS* p.270) that there were three classes of oars, thranite, zygian and thalamian, 62, 54 and 54 in number. Literature shows that these names were also applied to the oarsmen. There were then 170 oarsmen, the balance of the ship's company of 200 being made up of officers, petty officers and tradesmen, as well as marines and bowmen. The smaller number of the zygian and thalamian oarsmen is likely to have been the result of the contraction of the hull fore and aft.

(v) There is only one piece of evidence bearing on the speed of the trireme under oar, and this concerns a voyage and not the short bursts of speed required in battle. Xenophon, writing at the beginning of the 4th century, says that from Byzantium to Heracleia (on the south coast of the Black Sea) it is a long day's voyage for a trireme under oar. The distance is 140 miles, and there is a contrary current through the straits of about 4–5 knots; though once the ship had

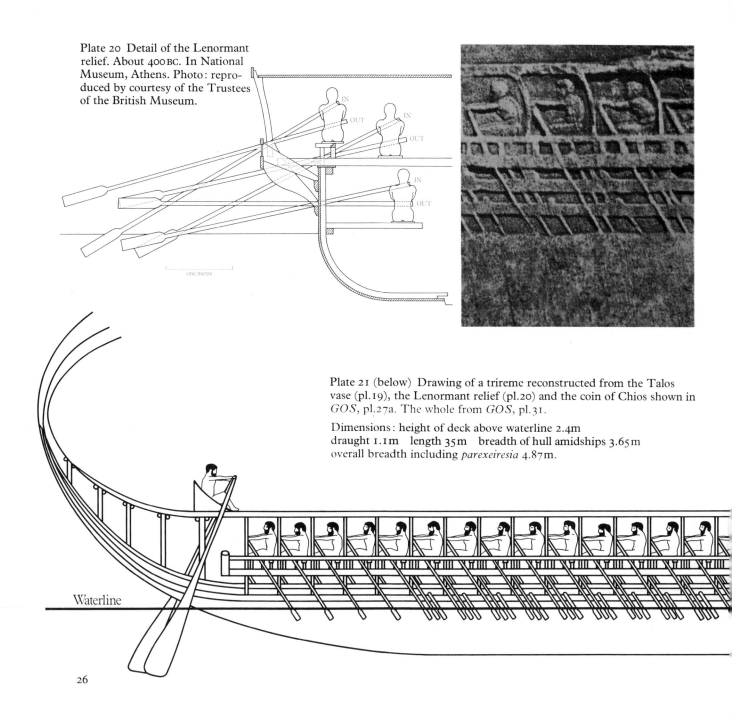

Plate 20 Detail of the Lenormant
relief. About 400 BC. In National
Museum, Athens. Photo: reproduced by courtesy of the Trustees
of the British Museum.

IN
OUT
IN
OUT
IN
OUT

one metre

Plate 21 (below) Drawing of a trireme reconstructed from the Talos
vase (pl.19), the Lenormant relief (pl.20) and the coin of Chios shown in
GOS, pl.27a. The whole from *GOS*, pl.31.

Dimensions: height of deck above waterline 2.4m
draught 1.1m   length 35m   breadth of hull amidships 3.65m
overall breadth including *parexeiresia* 4.87m.

Waterline

26

entered the Black Sea there would be a favourable current for the rest of the voyage.

It should be observed that the oar-system attributed to the trireme by almost all current books of reference, the *a zenzile* system as practised at Genoa and Venice (see Pl.22), is ruled out by the evidence given above. On this system three oarsmen sat side by side on a bench placed at an angle to the gunwale rowing oars, one each, which were nearly twice as long as those attested for the trireme. Eighty five oars a side arranged on this system cannot be accommodated in a ship 35 m long, the maximum length of the trireme. If the length of the oars is reduced to the 4 m attested for the trireme, the freeboard is necessarily reduced to a few centimetres.

On the basis of a projection from the Lenormant relief (Pl.20) it has been possible to make a model illustrating in three dimensions the oar system supported by this evidence (see above Pl.17) and to make a drawing of a complete trireme under oar (Pl.21). Diagrams illustrating the Italian *a zenzile* and *a scaloccio* oar-system employed in the Renaissance are given in Pls.22 and 23.

A number of characteristics of the trireme emerge from the accounts, two of them contemporary, of the invasion of mainland Greece by Xerxes in 480 BC,

culminating in the battle fought in the strait between Attica, which was in Persian occupation, and the island of Salamis to which the Greek naval forces had retreated. For the details of the campaign see *GOS* p.137–155. With the exception of a very few pente-contors all the ships on both sides were triremes.

The first of these characteristics is indicated by the operation of drying-out. Herodotus (VII 59^{2-3}) says that when the Persian fleet had assembled at Doriscus the captains took their ships to a beach near-by, 'pulled them up on the beach and dried them out'. Thucydides records the letter which Nicias, in the autumn of 414 BC, sent to the Athenian assembly. He was one of the generals in command of the expedition which had been dispatched to Sicily in the previous year. 'Our fleet', he writes, 'was at the outset in first-class condition, the ships dry and the crews unimpaired, but now the ships are waterlogged and the crews have deteriorated. It is not possible for us to beach the ships and dry them out, because the enemy fleet . . . keeps us continually on the look-out for an attack'. This

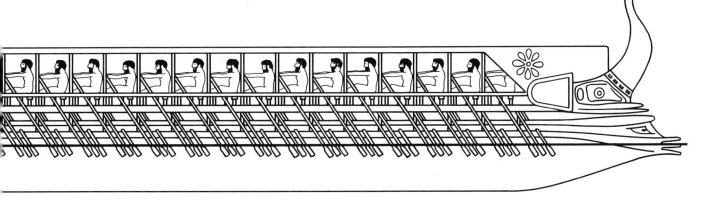

drying-out of the Persian fleet immediately before their descent on Greece seems to be the reason why it performed better than the Greek fleet and why this factor was recognized and accepted by both sides. In the first engagements at Artemisium, after the Persians had suffered great losses in a storm which caught them heading south along the inhospitable Magnesian coast but had succeeded in reaching Aphetae, the Greek captains tried in a preliminary skirmish to test their enemy's fighting tactics and his use of the '*diekplous*' or breakthrough. What this 'breakthrough' was is shown by Herodotus' account of the method by which the Phocaean naval tactician Dionysius trained the Ionian fleet when they were in revolt against the Persians in 494 BC. 'He took the fleet to sea,' Herodotus says (VI 11²–12²), 'regularly in line ahead to train the oarsmen by making the ships carry out a 'breakthrough' of each other's line . . .' The 'breakthrough' was then a manoeuvre by which ships in line ahead broke through

a squadron of ships in line abreast. To return to Artemisium, the Greek captains, realizing that their ships were the slower, adopted the defensive tactic against the 'breakthrough' and formed their ships in a close circle with bows pointing outwards. The Persian ships in line ahead, being thus unable to effect a 'breakthrough', carried out the consequential manoeuvre without realizing its danger, the *periplous* or encirclement of the Greek ships, which then 'exploded' their formation and destroyed some of the enemy ships by ramming them in the beam. The reason why the Greeks had not been able to dry out their ships as recently as the Persians had dried out theirs was presumably the same sort of reason that Nicias gave, that they were unable to risk their ships being out of commission when the Persians attacked. This recognized disadvantage of the Greek ships must be taken into account when the tactics of the final battle are assessed.

Plate 22 Diagram illustrating the Renaissance *a zenzile* oar system.

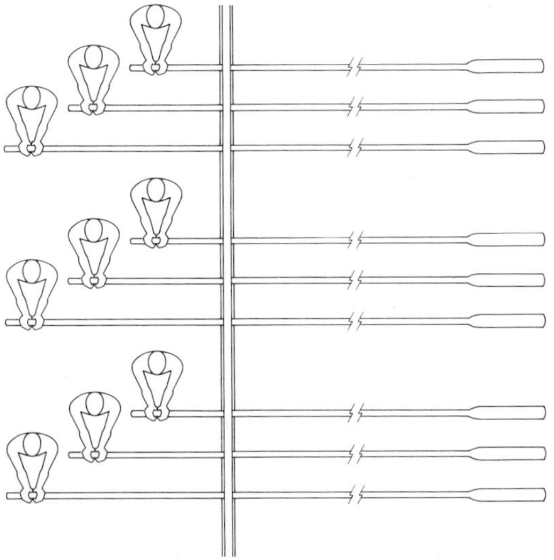

Plate 23 Diagram illustrating the Renaissance *a scaloccio* oar system.

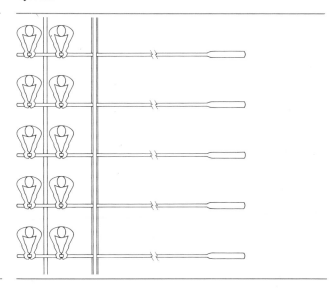

The second characteristic arises from a minor difference between the two fleets. In general the ships on both sides seem to have been very similar, at least in silhouette. A Persian squadron, arriving late at Aphetae, mistook a Greek patrol for their own ships. In silhouette therefore the Phoenician, Egyptian and Ionian ships of the Persian fleet must have been identical to those of the Greek allies. But it seems that there was a difference in manning which probably accompanied a structural difference. Thucydides remarked (I 14³) that 'the ships with which the Athenians fought at Salamis were not yet decked throughout (*dia pases*)'. Foster Smith (Loeb edition) translates the Greek phrase as 'throughout their length', but Torr and Casson are undoubtedly right in rendering the phrase 'throughout their breadth' i.e. 'right across'. Thucydides' remark implies that later Athenian triremes were decked 'right across'; and Casson (p.87) links the remark with a passage in Plutarch's *Life of Cimon* (xii 2). When Cimon was operating in Ionian waters in 467 BC with a joint Athenian and East Greek naval force, he had 'taken over a fleet which had been well constructed by Themistocles for speed and manoeuvreability and had made the ships broader and decked them right across so that they might attack the enemy with greater offensive power of many armed men'. The reason why the trireme was decked right across was then to accommodate more armed men on deck, and the converse is implied, that the narrow deck meant that only a few armed men could be accommodated. Now it is the case that the ships of the Chians at the battle of Lade in the Ionian revolt in 495 BC are said (Herodotus VI 15¹) to have carried 40 *epibatai* (armed men on deck), and the ships of Xerxes' fleet in 480 BC are said (Herodotus VII 18²) to have had 30 Persian, Median and Sacan *epibatai*. And these were in addition to the *epibatai* which they would normally carry. The Athenian *epibatai* at Salamis, on the other hand, were

much fewer. The Themistocles decree (see *GOS* p.122–127) gives ten *epibatai* and four bowmen, Plutarch, probably mistakenly, gives 14 *epibatai* and four bowmen. It looks therefore as if it was an East Aegean practice to have a broad deck and many deck soldiers; and that when the Chians joined the Athenian fleet after Salamis, Cimon adopted the practice of his new allies and had to enlarge the decks to accommodate the additional men. The conclusion then is that at Salamis the Athenian ships certainly, and probably those of the other Greek allies as well, were lightly built with a narrow deck and few *epibatai*, whereas the ships of the Persian fleet were more top-heavy with a deck right across, that is to say, covering the outriggers as well as the hull and a great many deck soldiers on it. It is an interesting confirmation of this conclusion that the earliest of our three pieces of evidence for the trireme at Athens, the Vienna fragment (Pl.18), should show a narrow deck and the later two (Pls. 19 and 20) should show a broad one. The two-level long ships on the Nineveh reliefs (see above Pl.14a and b) undoubtedly had a narrow deck, and so does the two-level long ship etched on the Ficoronian chest in the Villa Giulia at Rome (Casson pl.104 end of the 5th century).

The two characteristics noted seem at first sight to be contradictory. The Persian ships move better in the water, yet are top-heavy and are more heavily built, whereas the Greek ships are more lightly built, yet move less well in the water. These contradictions, which are readily explicable, also appear in the accounts of the battle. In the debate which took place on the night before the engagement, Themistocles argued against the proposal of the Spartan commander Eurybiades to take the ships back to the isthmus of Corinth where the army had already retired. 'If we fight there' Herodotus reports him as saying 'it will be in the open sea which is least advantageous to us since our ships are heavier and fewer in number'. The Greek ships, although more lightly built and having fewer soldiers on deck, were in fact at this moment heavier than the ships of the Persian fleet because they needed drying out, while the Persian ships, in spite of their more heavily built deck and greater weight of deck-soldiers, were in fact lighter at that moment, because they had just dried out. Plutarch, writing of the battle itself five centuries later, says: 'As usual at the hour of dawn a breeze sprang up blowing through the straits from the sea, which did not harm the Greek ships which were low in the water but was fatal to the Persian ships which had high sterns and decks and greater momentum'. Plutarch is thinking in terms of the ships of his own day which (as we shall see below p.36) differed in height, to explain the contrast which he must have found in his sources between the top-heaviness of the Persian ships and the lighter build and lower centre of gravity of the Greek ships. This contrast is perfectly reconcilable with an identity of silhouette.

Plate 24 Map of the Salamis battle area. From *GOS*, map 3.

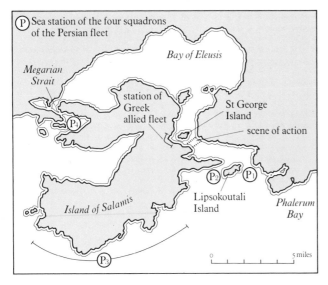

The third characteristic which emerges is a pretty obvious one, the importance of the fatigue factor. By a simple but effective intelligence operation Themistocles succeeded in persuading the enemy that the Greeks were on the point of making a night withdrawal to the isthmus from the beaches of Paloukia bay (see Pl.24) (just in fact what the Spartan commander had been urging them to do). At sunset, Aeschylus says, at midnight according to Herodotus, Xerxes manned his four squadrons and sent them to sea. One was ordered to close the western escape route by the Megarian channel, two to close the eastern channels on each side of the island now called Lipsokoutali, and the fourth to patrol the outer coast of the island of Salamis. After a night at the oar the two eastern squadrons penetrated the straits to reconnoitre the Paloukia beaches which they expected to find deserted. As they moved in, the Greek fleet put to sea with crews that had enjoyed a night's rest and emerged from behind the small island of St George to meet the weary and surprised Persian squadrons crowded into the narrow strait and thus unable to bring their full numbers to bear. The fatigue factor had turned the tables, and the Greeks were in a position to effect a 'breakthrough' on the right wing, where they had the support of a friendly shore, and follow it up with an 'encirclement'.

The Salamis campaign illustrated very vividly the opportunities which the trireme offered to a naval commander of genius, and its efficiency as a weapon of war given the right conditions. It illustrates vividly, too, the weakness of the trireme. The great losses, even if we take Herodotus' figure of 400 ships with a grain of salt, which the Persians suffered on the coasts of Magnesia and Euboea, show its vulnerability to bad weather. The accepted tactical position at Artemisium shows its rapid deterioration if kept at sea for any length of time without drying-out. The final battle also underlines the importance of the fatigue factor. It hardly needs to be stated that sail plays no part in battle performance. Sails were normally left on shore when a battle was imminent.

During the period of roughly 50 years which separates the second Persian invasion from the outbreak of the Peloponnesian war between Athens and Sparta the fleet of the Greek allies, which had been joined by the ships of the Greek cities of Asia Minor, ruled the Aegean. This fleet soon became an instrument of Athenian policy in the exercise of a political hegemony. Phoenician fleets, which were its only rivals, were defeated and destroyed first at Mycale, then in 469 at the river Eurymedon, and finally in 451 off Cyprus. No Phoenician ships entered Greek waters again for 40 years. As we have seen, the Themistoclean concept of the trireme as an offensive weapon in itself came to be modified through East Aegean influence towards the concept of the long ship as a platform for armed men, what Thucydides later called the 'old-fashioned type of sea-fighting'. But the engagements of the Peloponnesian war show that the Themistoclean concept remained the orthodox one.

Athenian hegemony, based on a trireme fleet and on the skill of the oarsmen and the resource of the commanders who manned it, was brought to an end when Athens overreached herself in attempting to attack and besiege an equally vigorous and democratic city far from her home base. The Syracusans, with help from Athens' enemies in mainland Greece, succeeded in containing the Athenian fleet within the Great Harbour where, with no room for a 'breakthrough' or 'encirclement', the skill of the Athenian oarsmen and steersmen was fatally handicapped. In battle the ships had to meet head-on, and the inventive Corinthians had discovered, just before the final battles in the Great Harbour, a structural modification in the bow area which could under favourable circumstances reduce the Athenian advantage of skill. Thucydides (VII 34[5]) relates an inconclusive but significant engagement at the entrance to the Corinthian Gulf between a Corinthian squadron and the Athenian squadron based on Naupactus, in which seven Athenian ships had been put out of action. They had been rammed head-on and their outriggers smashed and forced back by ships equipped with specially reinforced *epotides* (see above p.23), i.e. projecting transverse beams in the bows shielding the outriggers. The Syracusans appear to have been quick to learn the lesson of this engagement, and Thucydides describes how they 'shortened the bows of their ships and strengthened them by laying stout *epotides* on their bows and fixing stays to the ships' sides both inside and out'. The Athenians were forced to adopt similar measures, making their ships heavier. And finally they crowded all the available fighting men on to the decks of their remaining ships. Driven thus to negate all the structural and tactical principles on which their naval superiority had been based, they were crushingly defeated.

Although in the century which followed her defeat in Sicily Athens employed her fleet of triremes in successful battles as well as in unsuccessful ones, and had admirals of distinction in Conon, Chabrias, Iphicrates and Timotheus, the exploitation of her skill in rowing and fighting the trireme never again led to a political hegemony or restored her former prosperity. When she adopted the new types of warship in the second half of the 4th century she did so cautiously: 18 quadriremes among 492 triremes in 330–329 BC, and five years later seven quinqueremes and 50 quadriremes. Her caution was perhaps partly based on a sentimental attachment to the type which had been the key to her greatness. The new types appear in the naval lists after the old one. But it was certainly also partly based on economic weakness.

The Age of the Polyremes

Note on terminology : It was reasonable when speaking of the long ships of the 5th century to use the latin-based English word 'trireme' for the ship the Greeks called 'trieres', and 'quadrireme' and 'quinquereme' for the ships the Greeks called 'tetreres' and 'penteres'. But the higher denominations do not always have latin-based English words to denote them. It is proposed therefore that in this and subsequent chapters the series 'threes' (triremes), 'fours' (quadriremes), 'fives' (quinquereremes) and so on should be adopted, since this is the only series which can be consistently applied. It is also quite explicit in describing ships with three, four or more files of oarsmen on each side of the ship.

I 'Fours' 'Fives' and 'Sixes'

There seems to be no good reason for disbelieving Diodorus' categorical statement, twice repeated (xiv 41 3,42 2,44 7), that Dionysius I of Syracuse, preparing for war with the Carthaginians in 398 BC, built 'fours' and 'fives' 'the latter not having yet been constructed at this time'. The implication with regard to the 'four' is that this type had been previously built, and Pliny (*Natural History* 7 207) cites the weighty authority of Aristotle that it had been invented by the Carthaginians. Diodorus (xvi 44 6) speaks of 'fives' at Sidon in 351/0 and Arrian (ii 21 9,22 2) relates that when Tyre was attacked by Alexander in 332 her first line ships consisted of three 'fives' and seven 'threes', while the Cypriot kings, Pnytagoras, Androcles and Panicrates, had fleets of 'fives'. As we have seen, in the naval lists at Athens for 330/29 (IG 2² 1627 22) 18 'fours' appear for the first time, after the 492 'threes'

and before the triacontors, an interesting value-rating. Five years later the lists (IG 2² 1629 808) record 50 'fours' and seven 'fives'. The historian Aristobulus, who accompanied Alexander, is quoted by Arrian (vii 19 3) as saying that when Alexander arrived at Thapsacus on the Euphrates in 324 he found a fleet of two 'fives', three 'fours' and 12 'threes', part of which had been brought up the river by Neanthes and part transported overland from the Phoenician coast. Soon after the death of Alexander the defeat of Athens by a Macedonian/Phoenician fleet at the battle of Amorgus in 322 marked the end at the same time of Athenian naval ambitions and (until the Roman empire) of fleets composed largely of 'threes'. When Antigonus assembled a fleet of about 240 ships in 315 BC it was made up of 90 'fours', ten 'fives', three 'nines', ten 'tens' and 140 open ships (*aphractoi* Diodorus xix 62 8). The Phoenician ship excavated by Miss Honor Frost at Lilybaeum (modern Marsala) seems to be a good example of an aphract triacontor (open 30-oared ship) of the 4th century (Pl.25).

It is time to ask the question how the new types, of higher denomination than the 'three', could have been rowed. The answer still given in most of the books of reference is that of Tarn. He believed on grounds which now have to be rejected (see above p.27), that a 'three' employed a system known in Renaissance Italy as *a zenzile* (see Pl.22 above). He thought mistakenly that the Athenian naval lists provided evidence that at that time a 'four' was an expanded 'three', and a 'five' an expanded four, and consequently that 'fours' and 'fives' at their first introduction were rowed also on the *a zenzile* system, although as Rodgers pointed out the *a zenzile* system in Renaissance Italy was never so expanded. There is a very good reason why. The oars of an Italian 'three' were considerably longer than those attested for an ancient 'three'. The length was needed so that with that system the gunwale could be at a safe distance above the water, but the inner oars of a putative *a zenzile* 'four' or 'five' would have been too long altogether. Tarn proceeded to argue that at a later date the *a scaloccio* or 'staircase' system was adopted in

'fours' and 'fives' (see Pl.23), and later employed in all the larger polyremes. By this system in Renaissance Italy a number of men could work a single large oar, their rowing seats rising in steps from the gunwale to the middle line of the ship. His belief that by Roman times 'fours' and 'fives' had changed to this system was based on an interpretation of an incident related by Appian (*Civil War* 4 85) soon after the battle of Myndus in 42 BC. Octavian had sent his fleet under Salvidienus against Sextus Pompeius' ships in the strait of Messana. Pompeius' ships had the more experienced crews so that in the choppy waters of the

Plate 25 Drawing of the Marsala ship as reconstructed. End of 4th century BC. By courtesy of Miss Honor Frost.

straits they were less affected than Salvidienus' men 'who from inexperience could not stand up properly nor were able to get their oars out of the water nor could they use their rudder oars effectively'. Tarn claimed that this passage shows that Salvidienus' men rowed standing up and must therefore have been working long sweeps with four or five men on each. Casson (p.104) has explained the passage correctly. Appian is describing first the effect of the choppy sea on the men on deck (they could not keep their feet), then on the oarsmen (they caught crabs), and lastly on the steersman.

Although Tarn's gangs of four and five oarsmen are to be rejected as an explanation of the 'fours' and 'fives', nevertheless it is certain that the new types embodied a new principle, the use of more than one man to an oar and the consequent 'staircase', and that the most commonly used, and therefore the most efficient, new types, the 'four', 'five' and 'six' were simple developments of the 'two' and 'three' by double-manning of the oars at two or three levels. The rather puzzling types, the 'one-and-a-half' (*hemiolia*) and the 'three/one-and-a-half (*trihemiolia*) are probably to be explained straightforwardly as ships with three files across the ship at one level (so one-and-a-half files a side) for the *hemiolia*, and three files across the ship at two levels (so twice one-and-a-half files a side = three) for the *trihemiolia* (see Morrison (1979)). The median file would provide double manning for half the oars on the port side and half the oars on the starboard side (see below, p.35).

Athenaeus (V 203 e ff) quotes from the late 3rd century writer Callixenus a detailed description of Ptolemy Philopator's monster 'forty', which includes the statement that the longest, thranite, oars were of 38 cubits (nearly 17 m). Oars of such a length prove with certainty that multiple-manning had been introduced in the larger polyremes of the 3rd century BC. It is also undeniable that there are no representations of ancient ships with oars at more than three levels. The numerical denominator in the type-names must accordingly refer to something other than levels, although in the case of the 'three', three is also the number of levels. It seems reasonable to conclude that multiple-manning at levels up to three is the key to the oar-system of the new types.

For the new types then three principles may be accepted:

(i) that the numerical denominator refers to the number of fore-and-aft, horizontal files of oarsmen (Gr. *stoichoi, taxeis* Lat. *ordines*) or, by another way of looking at it, to the number of oarsmen to each vertical division of the ship, the *interscalmium* or room, as in Pausanias' description (I 29 1) of Antigonus Gonatas' 'nine' as being 'nine oarsmen deep from the deck' on each side of the ship.

(ii) that the files were at not more than three levels.

And *(iii)* that at one, two, or three levels there was multiple-manning of oars.

So far, so good. But to the more searching questions about the number of levels (one, two, or three) in the various types, and the number of men rowing oars *a scaloccio* at each level, there has been little more than guesswork, some of it probably right. Yet the literary sources taken together with the small amount of monumental and numismatic evidence which is relevant can produce some reasoned answers.

The categories 'aphract', 'cataphract' begin to be used in describing the fleets of the 4th century as we have seen. Thucydides uses the word of contemporary warships as opposed to the open long ships of the earlier period which were more like pirate craft (I 10[4]). Polybius uses the word also of armoured cavalry (30 25 9). The bigger ships, of the denomination four and upwards, are always 'cataphract'. The 'three' is sometimes 'cataphract' and sometimes not. The 'three/one-and-a-half' seems to have been 'cataphract'. The equivalent Latin words are *tecta* or *constrata* for 'cataphract' and *aperta* for 'aphract' (see Torr pp.51–52). Now in all the representations of large Hellenistic and Roman long ships the oarsmen are 'boxed-in', presumably to protect them from missiles and the weather; and the oars emerge either at two levels through a pronounced boxed in outrigger (see Pl.29 a and b, Pl.30 below) or at two or three levels without an outrigger (Pl.31 and 32 a and b, 27 and 28) except in the case of the wall painting at Pompeii (Pl.35a). An incident in a duel between the flagships of the opposing admirals, Agrippa and Papias, in the Roman civil wars indicates the effect of boxing-in the oarsmen. The ships were certainly 'cataphract', probably as flagships (see below p.39) 'sixes'. Appian (*Civil Wars* 5 107) describes what happened: Agrippa's ship rammed Papias' in the bows 'beside the *epotis*', and the water poured in. All the *thalamioi*, i.e. those in the lowest seats, were trapped, but the rest, i.e. those in the zygian and thranite positions, broke through the *catastroma* and escaped. The account implies that the *catastroma*, which earlier meant only the deck, was now taken to include also the permanent sidescreens (Torr pp. 51–52), so that the words *cataphractos*, *tecta*, *constrata*, which originally meant only 'decked' now seem to mean 'boxed-in' as well.

What clues are there to link these representations of cataphract long ships with the known types? We are lucky to have a rather rough graffito from Alba Fucentia, dated at the end of the 1st century BC or the beginning of the 1st century AD, which is labelled *navis tetreris longa*, that is to say, as a 'four' – the only ancient picture of a long ship to be given a rating label (Pl.26). No oars are shown, but the hull is long and low, at least no higher than that of a 'three' (Pl.21), and such as would accommodate two levels of double-manned oars. It is boxed in. Other cataphract two-level ships which may be 'fours' are shown on the Vatican relief from Praeneste (modern Palestrina) (Pl.27), the rough Naples frieze (Casson pl.119), and

Plate 26 Graffito of a Roman 'four' found at Alba Fucentia. End of 1st century BC or beginning of 1st century AD. From Casson, pl.126.

the British Museum tomb-relief (Pl.28). It is not clear whether the last is cataphract. If not, it may be one of those light open 'twos' which the Romans called liburnians (see p.37).

If the two-level cataphract ships without an outrigger are 'fours', what are the ships in which the oars at two-levels are rowed at both levels through a pronounced outrigger, i.e., the Lindus prow and the Samothrace prow (Pl.29 a and b) and the ship on the mosaic in the Palazzo Barberini at Palestrina (Pl.30)? There is some reason to believe (Blinkenberg (1938): Morrison (1979)) that these are 'three/one-and-a-halfs' (*trihemioliai*, p.34) since the Samothrace prow was dedicated by Rhodes and these ships seem to have been developed there. They appear in the Ptolemaic fleets, and the Palazzo Barberini mosaic depicts a scene on the Nile. They were also used in the Roman fleets where they ranked as cataphract.

In his poem on the Civil War the Roman poet Lucan (III 524 ff) describes a battle between Julius Caesar's admiral Decimus Brutus and the fleet of Massilia in

Plate 27 Relief from Palestrina in the Vatican Museum. 2nd half of 1st century BC. Photo: Vatican Museum.

Plate 28 Tomb relief in the British Museum. AD 100. Photo: reproduced by courtesy of the Trustees of the British Museum.

49 BC. He speaks of the wings of the Roman fleet being surrounded by ships of many kinds: (1) 'strong threes', (2) ships driven by 'a fourfold, rising, file of built-up oarsmen (*quater surgens exstructi remigis ordo*)' i.e. four files at more than one level (the building-up referring either to the second level, or to the double-manning, or generally to both), and (3) ships of more oars still. In an an account of the same engagement Caesar (*B.C.* I 56 1) gives the Massiliotes 17 warships 'of which eleven were *tectae*' i.e. cataphract, and thus confirms that they had at least 'fours' and 'fives'. It seems likely that Lucan's second category were 'fours', and it will be made clear as we proceed that the ships of his third category were 'fives'. Turning to the Roman fleet, Lucan speaks of liburnians 'content to have grown with twin files' (i.e. they were ships with two files of oarsmen on each side, one higher than the other) 'in a sickle shaped formation'. 'But higher than all is the flagship of Brutus, driven by six-fold beats (*senis verberibus*). 'It advances its mass upon the deep, and seeks the water from afar with its highest oars'.

The height of the deck of an oared long ship is determined by two factors: (1) the levels, one, two and three, at which the oars were rowed (and it should be observed that the thranite, zygian and thalamian oarports could apparently be arranged either *en echelon* i.e. ⋰⋰⋰, or one directly above the other i.e. ⦙ ⦙ ⦙, the latter arrangement necessitating a a higher deck than the former; (2) the steps in the rising 'staircase' of oarsmen's seats required by multiple-manning *a scaloccio* (see Pl.23). In the first place a ship in which oars were rowed at two levels with one man to each oar, if it had a deck, would have one higher than a ship with a single file on each side at one level. And a ship with three levels of oarsmen would naturally have a higher deck than ships with two. Once double-manning was adopted an additional factor appears to affect the height of the deck. The inner oarsman (i.e. the one nearer the middle line of the ship) had to sit a step higher than the outer oarsman because of the angle made by the oar with the water. Now if Lucan had given us a numerically increasing series of ships each higher than the last, we might have supposed that he was implying an oar system of single oars rowed by gangs of two, three, four, five and six oarsmen *a scaloccio*, i.e. that the reason for the additional height in each case was the additional step in the 'staircase'. (The possibility that he might have implied 2–6 *levels* is of course ruled out: see above, p. 34.) But he does not give us such a numerically increasing series. He speaks of liburnians

'content to have grown with twin files', a description which could imply either an *a scaloccio* 'staircase' of two steps or a ship with two levels of single-manned oars. There are reasons apart from Lucan's text for preferring the latter. 'Threes' he merely characterizes as 'strong', but there is no reason to think that they, like the Athenian fifth/fourth century 'threes', did not have three levels of single-manned oars. Then he speaks of ships driven 'by a fourfold rising file of built up oarsmen', a description which could imply a 'staircase' on which a gang of four men rowed a single large oar, or alternatively two levels of double-manned oars.

Plate 29
(*a*) (below) Prow at Lindus Rhodes. About 265–260 BC. Drawing after Blinkenberg *Triemiolia*, fig.7, p.30.
(*b*) (right) Prow on which the Nike of Samothrace stands. 200–180 BC. Louvre 2369. Photo: Musée du Louvre.

Plate 30 Detail of the mosaic in the Palazzo Barberini at Palestrina. Early 1st century BC. Photo: Vasari.

Evidence from the fourth century (*GOS* p.290) relating to the relative monetary value of the oars of a 'three' and of a 'four' favours the latter alternative; and it will be seen that facts about the relationship of the 'four' to the 'five' do the same. Lucan's description of the third category falls in place. It has more oars than the 'four'. This statement is unlikely to mean that additional oars were employed by making the same number of files longer, because it appears that the files in a 'five' were about the same length as the files of a 'three' (see below, p.41) and the length of the files of the 'four' are likely to have been the same. The conclusion follows that if a 'five' had more oars the reason was that it had three levels as opposed to the 'four's' two.

'Sixfold beats' is an obscure phase to use of the rowing of a ship in which six files of oarsmen on each side rowed in some fashion *a scaloccio*, but it is paralleled in the indiscriminate use of *ordines remigum* (files of oarsmen) and *ordines remorum* (files of oars), on one occasion in the same paragraph by Roman writers (Florus II 21 5: see Casson, p.98 n.10) to mean the same thing, the fore-and-aft files of oarsmen. The phrase seems to be latin for one of the greek *-krotos* series, *monokrotos* (single beat), *dikrotos* (double beat), *trikrotos* (triple beat) up to *hexkaidekakrotos* (sixteen beat) used of ships with one, two, three . . . sixteen files of oarsmen on each side of the ship. Lucan must mean that Brutus' ship was a 'six', which was in fact the usual type for a flagship. It is higher than all the other ships, and it has three levels of oars, not two, since some of them are 'highest'. If it has three levels and is higher than a 'three', as he says, it must have had another reason than the three levels for its height. It appears from Roman representations of the larger three-level ships (e.g. on the late 2nd century BC Calenian bowl Viereck Pl.17 and below Pls.31 and 32a, 32b) that the oarports in these ships are not as in the 'threes' at three levels *en echelon* but one directly above

the other, an arrangement which would have added to the height. Double-manning at the thranite level in the 'six' would also entail a higher deck than single-manning at that level in the 'three'. The Roman portraits of ships with three levels of oars arranged one directly above the other also show no outrigger. Absence of an outrigger would also entail longer oars than in the 'three'. Consideration of the precise nature of the oar-system of a 'five' must be deferred. Lucan merely says that the 'five' had more oars than a 'four' (and this would be the case if its additional file on each side was at a third level), and that it was lower than a 'six'.

There is a story in Polybius which seems to have a bearing on the relationship between the 'four' and the 'five' (1 47 5, 59 8). During the siege of Lilybaeum in the first Punic War (264–241) a specially well-built Rhodian 'four' was captured by the Romans and later served as a model for the 200 'fives' built by the Romans for their naval offensive in 242, which resulted in the victory off the Aegates islands and brought the war to an end. The truth of this story should not be doubted on the ground that it looks like a doublet of the story that a captured Punic cataphract was the model for Rome's first 'five' in 261 (Polybius 1 20 15). In any case the story shows that Polybius knew that

Plate 31 Relief at Ostia. 2nd half of the 1st century BC. Photo: Vasari.

the hull dimensions and design of 'fives' and 'fours' were sufficiently similar for the story to be plausible.

What else may be discovered about the relationship of 'fours' to 'fives'? Polybius, Livy and Appian relate an incident which occurred in 203 BC as the Second Punic War was drawing to its close. Envoys were returning to the Roman camp in Africa in a 'five' from Carthage. When the two escorting Punic 'threes' turned back, the Roman 'five' was attacked by three Punic 'fours' out of Utica. Livy (xxx 26 6) says: 'These could not make a strike with the ram by reason of the 'five's' speedy avoiding tactics, nor could the marines leap from the decks of the lower ships on to the deck of the higher ship, which put up an excellent defence while its missiles lasted'. Polybius (15 2 12), writing more than a century earlier than Livy, calls the Punic ships 'threes' and does not say anything about the

relative height of the ships, nor does Appian (*Pun.*6 33). But, whichever account we prefer, the important thing is what Livy in the 1st century BC knew about the relative height of 'fours' and 'fives', and Livy, as Tarn once observed, had an excellent grasp of nautical matters. If then a 'five's' deck was so much higher than a 'four's' that marines could not leap from one to the other, it is a matter of more than the few inches of height which one step in the 'staircase' would imply. If a 'four' was rowed at two levels, as seems likely, then a 'five' was rowed at three, a conclusion already reached in connexion with the Lucan passage (above p.36). But two questions remain to be settled. If the oars of the 'five' were double-manned at two levels and single-manned at one, at which level did the single-manning occur? And were the different levels of oars *en echelon* as in the 'three' and 'four', or one directly above the other as appears to be the case in the 'six'? Casson, without giving reasons, assigns the single-manning to the thalamian (lowest) oars. Against this is the inference from Polybius (see

Plate 32 (*a*) and (*b*) Reliefs of three-level oared ships found at Pozzuoli. 1st century BC–1st century AD. (*a*) with *parodos* (*b*) without *parodos*. Photo: della Superintendenze alle Antichitá delle Province di Napoli e Caserta.

p.39 above) that the 'five' was a 'four' minimally modified, and possibly a similar inference from Lucan who merely says that the 'five' had more oars than a 'four'. These considerations do not form a strong argument, but there are as far as I know no decisive factors on either side. The inference from Polybius again is in favour of the oars of a 'five' being arranged at the different levels *en echelon* as in the 'four': and Lucan's emphasis on the greater height of the 'six' than all the other types including the 'five' tells in the same direction. The weight of probability is then in favour of a 'five' with oars at three levels *en echelon* and thranite oars single-manned and accordingly rowed through an outrigger as in the 'three'. The external view of such a vessel would then be hardly distinguishable from that of a 'three'.

The number of oarsmen in a 'four' is nowhere given, but Polybius (1 26 7) gives the oarsmen of a Roman 'five' at the battle of Ecnomus (256BC) as 300 with 120 marines. Two files of *thalamioi*, two of *zygioi* and one of *thranitai* on each side, with an average of 30 in each file would give 300 oarsmen in all. These figures bear comparison with the numbers for the files in an Athenian 'three' in the fourth century (IG 2² 1615–1618) i.e. 27 *thalamioi*, 27 *zygioi* and 31 *thranitai* on each side. Given the same sort of disparity between the files at different levels the numbers for a 'five' might have been, on each side, 2×29, 2×29, $34 = 150$, and the total number of oars on each side 92. If the relationship of the 'four' to the 'five' is as Polybius suggests, then the number of oarsmen on each side in a 'four' would have been 116, and the number of oars 58. The rather tentative inference in *GOS* (p.291) that a 'four's' oars were about a third fewer than a 'three's' (85 on each side) seems to be confirmed.

There is no evidence that any new slipways were constructed at Athens when the 'fours' and 'fives' were introduced after the middle of the fourth century BC. It is likely, but not of course certain, that they were

accommodated in the Zea shipsheds, built originally for 'threes' 37m long and just under 6m broad (*GOS* p.183). The breadth of a 'five' is deducible from the account of the prows of 'fives' used to make the pyre of Hephaestion in Diodorus (see *GOS* 285–6). It is 5m, which with thranite files of 34 oarsmen would have fitted comfortably into the shipsheds. It may perhaps be noted that the calculation of the length and breadth of an *a zenzile* 'five', as proposed by Tarn, is 40m by 6.5m, much too large for the ship-sheds (Wallinga p.78). Under the empire, the number of men in the files of a 'five' may have been increased to an average of 40, since Pliny (*N.H.*32 1 4) says that Caligula's 'five' had 400 oarsmen. Since the ship was Caligula's flagship it may actually have been a 'six'.

Diodorus mentions (xx 112 4) that in 302 a 'six' which was the flagship of Cassander's admiral Pleistarchus, while sailing to the support of Lysimachus, was lost in a storm with 500 men on board. A Roman 'five', 50 years later at Ecnomus, carried 120 deck soldiers. Forty of those were what Thiel calls the 'garrison', i.e. the normal sea-going complement, while the other 80 were legionaries put on board for the engagement. Since Pleistarchus was bringing military support to Lysimachus it is likely that he was carrying all the troops he could accommodate on a sea-voyage. The number of 500 can, at a guess, be made up by six files of 35 oarsmen each on an average on each side (420 all told) with 60 deck soldiers and the usual 20 *hyperesia* (see *GOS* p.266 ff). The files on each side may in fact have been: thranite 2×37, zygian 2×32, thalamian 2×32. The 'six' would then have been a little longer than the 'five'. It need not have been any broader, but its deck, for the reasons given, would have been higher. It would have needed no outrigger.

The earliest appearance of the 'six' is in Dionysius II's fleet at Syracuse in 356BC (Aelian *Var.Hist.* vi 12). This is quite credible since the 'six' is a logical development of the 'five' which had been invented at Syracuse by his father. Pliny confirms that the 'six' was invented there (*N.H.* 7 207). In 289 BC Agathocles had 'sixes' in the fleet he assembled against Carthage (Diodorus xxi 16 1). It so happens that in the middle of the 4th century a series of coins begins to which M.Basch (1969) has drawn attention (see Pl.33 a and b). They derive from Aradus on the Phoenician coast, and appear to portray open-sided three-level ships. These ships are to be contrasted with the ordinary 'three', on the contemporary coin from Sidon (Pl.33 c). Remarkably similar to the ships on these coins is an Egyptian ship-model dated about the end of the century, now in Copenhagen (Pl.34). Neither the model nor the Aradus coins show outriggers. M.Basch believes that these ships represent a Phoenician version of a 'three' going back to the 7th century (Basch p.230 ff). G.F.Bass (Pl.4 note) has suggested more plausibly that the Copenhagen model represents one of the big Hellenistic polyremes. It is of crude workmanship, but that fact may not entirely explain the thick stubs which are what remains of the oars. It could well be a 'six' or one of the larger polyremes employing three or more men to an oar at three levels. This type would be something which an Egyptian might wish to celebrate with a dedicated model and which a Phoenician city might boast on its coins.

II   The larger polyremes

(i) Their rise and fall

The adoption of double-manning in long ships at the beginning of the 4th century BC had led to 'fours', probably at Carthage, and then at Syracuse first to 'fives' and then to 'sixes'. Reason has been given for supposing that these three types were of the same order of magnitude as the 'three', as far as the hull measurements were concerned. The 'four' appears to have been lower, the 'six' a little higher than the

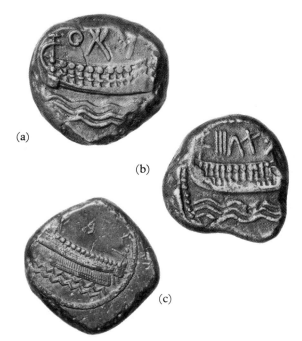

Plate 33 (*a*) and (*b*) Coins from Aradus in Phoenicia in the British Museum. 350–300 BC. (*c*) Coin of Sidon. About 373 BC. Also in the British Museum. Photos: reproduced by courtesy of the Trustees of the British Museum.

'three', while the 'five' is likely to have been about the same height. The length of the files of oarsmen, and hence the overall length, appears to have been roughly similar in all four types. The 'four' with four files across the ship (at each of two levels) is likely to have had a slightly broader hull than the 'three', and the 'five' and 'six' similarly. Neither the 'four' nor the 'six' would have needed an outrigger. If the 'five' was a 'three' with the thalamian and zygian oars double-manned, an outrigger would have been needed for the thranite oars, but there is no representation which can be identified as a 'five'. The *trihemiolia* as developed at Rhodes at the end of the 3rd century BC appears to have employed a mixture of single- and double-manning and to have been a powerful ship but smaller than the ordinary 'three', with shorter files and a narrower hull but in compensation substantial boxed-in outriggers.

In the competitive building programmes of Dionysius and his son at Syracuse there is a foretaste of the naval rivalries of the Hellenistic kings, the successors of Alexander. But the developments at Carthage and Syracuse were modifications of the 'three' probably motivated initially by the exigencies of the labour market in skilled oarsmen rather than prestigious increases in oar-power dictated by military or political ambitions. Antigonus, the father of Demetrius Poliorketes, began in earnest the expansion of the oared galley when he assembled a fleet of about 240 ships in 314 BC to challenge Egyptian naval supremacy. This fleet included, besides a large force of 'fours' and ten 'fives', three 'nines', ten 'tens' and 130 aphracts in addition. However, when Demetrius successfully led the Macedonian fleet against Ptolemy I's 'fours' and 'fives' in an engagement off Cypriot Salamis in 307, the higher denominations appear to have been left behind, either because they were not yet regarded as sufficiently proven or because Ptolemy was in any case outclassed. The seven Phoenician 'sevens', one of which was Demetrius's flagship, and the ten 'sixes' of the Macedonian fleet were the biggest ships present (Diodorus xx 49 2, 50 1). When two years later Demetrius attacked Rhodes, he is said to have had a fleet 'of all sizes' (Diodorus xx 82 4). Theophrastus (*Historia Plantarum* v 81: Torr p.7) speaks of unusually long timber cut by Demetrius in Cyprus for an 'eleven', which as Torr argues must belong to the period after the battle of Salamis which gave him control of the island. Plutarch attributes the invention of 'thirteens', 'fifteens' and 'sixteens' to him (*Demetrius* 20 and 31). Ptolemy II (Philadelphus, who succeeded Demetrius's opponent in 285) appears to have entered the building race with enthusiasm. The list of his ships

in Athenaeus (v 203 c), probably deriving from the Alexandrian writer Callixenus of Rhodes (end of 3rd century BC), gives, in the category of the biggest ships, two 'thirties', one 'twenty', four 'thirteens', two 'twelves', fourteen 'elevens', thirty 'nines', thirty-six 'sevens', five 'sixes' and seventeen 'fives'. An inscription shows that the two largest types were built in Cyprus probably by a Pyrgoteles, and the 'nines' and 'tens' are confirmed by mention in papyri (Casson Ch.Six App.2, note 17, p.140). Lysimachus, king of Thrace, made a remarkable contribution to the naval building competition with an 'eight', built at Heracleia, which by dint of great length could compete successfully with the larger denominations (Memnon Frg.13: Jacoby FGrH 434,8,5). It appears to have been responsible for the victory of Lysimachus' successor, Ptolemy Keraunos, over Demetrius' son, Antigonus Gonatas. The naval supremacy in the eastern Mediterranean which had now reverted to Egypt was left unchallenged until 246 BC when the aged Antigonus in alliance with Rhodes inflicted a series of defeats on the Egyptian admirals, first at Andros and then through the Rhodians off Ephesus, and finally at Cos. No account of these battles has survived, but Antigonus' flagship, the *Isthmia*, is described as *triarmenos* (see below p.45) and is probably to be identified with the ship of 'nine oars-

Plate 34 Model of a Hellenistic polyreme in the National Museum, Copenhagen, found at Erment in Egypt. End of the 4th century BC. Photo: National Museum, Copenhagen.

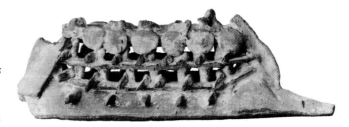

men deep from the deck' seen by Pausanias at Delos (Plutarch *Mor.* 676 d: Pollux i 85: Pausanias I 29 1. Tarn 1910. 216-8). I cannot agree with Casson's interpretation (1969. p.193) by which it would be a 'twenty-five'. Such monsters were never taken into battle. Meanwhile, in the western Mediterranean, Rome was fighting Carthage, in what ultimately turned into a naval war, for the possession of Sicily. The ships in this theatre of war were generally no larger than 'fives', although at Ecnomus in 256 both the Roman consuls had 'sixes' as their flagships (Polybius I 26 11).

The culmination, or perhaps the *reductio ad absurdum*, of the naval ambitions of the Hellenistic kings is the double-hulled 'forty' of Ptolemy IV Philopator (221–204) which, like all the ships of high denomination, was not a serious military proposition. At the end of the 3rd century there was rivalry in the Aegean between Attalus of Pergamum, in alliance with Rhodes, and Philip V of Macedon, which resulted in an indecisive action off Chios in 201. Philip's 53 cataphracts included his flagship, a 'ten', and lesser types down to 'fours', with *trihemioliai* and light craft as well. On the other side the only ships mentioned are 'fives', a 'three' and *trihemioliai* (Polybius 16 2 ff). Later, after Rome had entered the war in alliance with Attalus and Rhodes, a 'sixteen', 'of almost unmanageable size' as Livy describes it, is mentioned in the peace terms of 188 BC as a weapon Philip is allowed to keep (xxxiii 30 5,xlv 35 3.Cf. Polybius 18 44 6, and Plutarch *Aemilius Paulus* 30). Could Roman contempt go further?

Rome and Rhodes defeated Antiochus of Syria in 190 in two engagements fought off the coast of Asia Minor (Livy xxxvii 23 ff). In the first, Antiochus's fleet is said to have consisted of 37 ships 'of larger size' (*maioris formae*), including three 'sevens' and four 'sixes' (the remaining ships in this category being, pre- sumably, 'fives' and 'fours'), and, as 'ships of smaller size', ten 'threes'. This fleet was engaged successfully

by a Rhodian fleet of 30 'fours' and four 'threes'. Then, in a major action, a combined Roman/Rhodian fleet of 80 ships fought a larger enemy fleet of 89 ships including five 'of the largest size', i.e. three 'sixes' and two 'sevens'. The solidity of the Roman 'fives' and the fighting qualities of the Roman marines on their decks on the one hand, and the quickness and skilled oars- manship of the Rhodian ships on the other, led to the defeat of Antiochus.

The bigger polyremes were now on the way out, and there is no mention of them in the naval operations against Mithradates in the 1st century BC. Rome was content with the 'fives' with which she had defeated the Carthaginians, using the odd 'six' as a flagship. A 'six' in that capacity is attributed to Decimus Brutus, as we have seen, by Lucan in a description of his battle with the fleet of Massilia in 49 BC. At the battle of Myndus in 42 a skilled and nimble Rhodian fleet was defeated by the heavier Roman ships of the murderers of Caesar, Brutus and Cassius. In 39 Sextus Pompeius came to meet Octavian and Antony at Misenum in 'a fine 'six'' (Appian 5 70) while there were 'sixes' in Octavian's fleet in 36. In the sea-battles which led to the defeat of Sextus at Mylae and Naulochus there is only mention of 'heavy' ships in Octavian's fleet and 'light' ships in Sextus's, with no denominations given (Appian 5 96 ff). It is most unlikely that they included anything larger than a 'six'. A new development at this time, emphasizing the importance of the missile, was the construction on deck of light defensive structures, which could be jettisoned at need (Appian 5 118 and 121).

The period of complex naval competition which began with the defeat of Athens at Amorgus terminates in a final battle fought at Actium between Antony and Octavian in 31 BC. On the one side was the fleet with which Octavian had finally secured the defeat of Sextus in Sicilian waters. It had then been called 'heavy' in contrast to Sextus's fleet. On the other was an Aegean/Egyptian fleet under Antony and Cleopatra. Dio (L 23) says that Antony, realizing that Sextus had been beaten by the size of Octavian's ships and by the number of deck soldiers he could consequently deploy in battle, built ships which were of much higher denomination than the enemy's, i.e. few 'threes', but 'fours' and 'tens' and all the types in between. As Tarn observed, ships of higher denomination than ten had been built, but never in fact had seen action. The great *Leontophoros* of Lysimachus, which had, was of course technically an 'eight' albeit an extraordinarily long one. There is not much information about the ships in Octavian's fleet. Florus (II 21 6 = 4 11) says that they went up to 'sixes', which is exactly what one would expect. The idea that Octavian's fleet consisted of light liburnians ('twos') is a misinterpretation of a passage in Horace (Ep.I 1); but if his largest vessel was a 'six', probably the flagship, his fleet as a whole would have been lighter and faster, and also, as Dio says, in the main lower in the water, though the ships were well protected from missiles. Antony's fleet was a dinosaur surviving uncomfortably from an earlier age. Its decisive defeat meant that the larger polyremes, 'sevens' to 'tens', were never built again. There are none in the lists of the established Roman fleets of the imperial period (see below, p.47).

(ii) The nature of the larger polyremes

Lucan's description of the 'six' showed that it was a ship of three levels of oarsmen, that the oars rowed at the top level were longer than the others (so no outrigger), and that it rode higher in the water than 'threes', 'fours' and 'fives'. It was suggested that the reason why its deck was higher than the deck of 'threes' and 'fives' was on the one hand the abandonment of the *en echelon* arrangement of oar levels and on the other the double-manning of oars at the thranite level. Ships of denomination seven to nine require: three men at one level and two men at the other two; three men at two levels and two at the third; and three men at all three levels, while those of denomination ten to twelve require four men to each oar at one level and three at the other two levels (for a 'ten'), and four men at each of three levels (for a 'twelve'). In the case of the 'six' we have inferred three levels, and our information about the 'forty' at the other end of the scale also suggests three levels, since thranite oars are mentioned. It is perhaps reasonable to suppose that the types in between also had three levels, but it should be emphasized that information about these types is lacking. All we have is a number of representations of ships with oars at three levels. The implication of the lack is perhaps the likelihood that they all looked alike from the outside.

Antony's fleet at Actium in 31 BC had ships up to 'tens' according to Dio, up to 'nines' according to Florus. Orosius (vi 19), making the point that Antony's ships made up in size what they lacked in numbers, gives the information that they were 'in height ten feet from the water' (2.96m). Now the Lenormant relief (above Pl.20), showing a file of realistically drawn thranite oarsmen, thus provides a scale on which the height of the deck of a 'three' may be calculated, i.e. 8ft (2.4m). If then Orosius' information is reliable, a 'ten' or a 'nine', both probably with three men at each thranite oar, was not more than 0.6m higher in the water than a 'three'.

Antigonus' flagship at the battle of Cos (246 BC), the *Isthmia*, which we have reason to believe was a 'nine', is described as *triarmenos*, a word meaning 'three-fitted', which is usually translated 'three-decked'. This meaning would well fit the arrangement of oarports one directly above the other suggested by the Ostia and Pozzuoli reliefs (Pls.20 and 21).

An interesting point about Ptolemy Philopator's 'forty' is that its breadth is given by Callixenus as 'from side-gangway (*parodos*) to side-gangway', an expression which implies that there was no outrigger and confirms the assumption made above that the outrigger would be abandoned when the thranite oars were manned by more than one oarsman. Such a side-gangway is visible on a number of Hellenistic and Roman long ships (see e.g. Pl.27). The twin hulls of the 'forty' were each about 8.5m broad making a total breadth of 17m. It could thus have had 14 men at one level to each oar and 13 at the other two. There is only one possible explanation, that the gangs of 13 and 14 must have been divided into two, with one section pushing and the other pulling, all standing up, as is attested in galleys of modern times (see Rodgers p.258 Fig.34). The arrangement would be comfortably accommodated in the vertical and horizontal space provided. This method of rowing must have been used not only in the 'forty', but also in the 'twenty' and 'thirty'. It is not very surprising that the 'forty', in Plutarch's words, 'moved unsteadily and laboriously' and was only used for prestige purposes. Casson (p.108–112) has suggested that the oars of the 'forty' were worked not only over the outer sides of the linked hulls but over the inner sides as well. The hulls must then be about 12m apart yet be rigidly linked together, if that is possible, at bow and stern. He has then to suppose that the inner oarsmen on the port side of one hull row with their oars interweaved with the oars of the starboard oarsmen of the other hull, an arrangement which would appear to be a recipe for disaster. If they are not to interweave, the distance between the hulls must be increased to 20m. On the other hand two hulls closely attached would produce a ship of great stability in spite of a high centre of gravity. Huge loads of hay and straw are carried on closely linked twin hulls on the Nile at the present time.

There is one other of the big polyremes about which we have information. Lysimachus's 'eight' was built at Heracleia, possibly in emulation of Demetrius's 'sixteen' and 'fifteen' which he is said once to have inspected. It is described in a fragment of Memnon, who wrote a history of Heracleia in the reign of Trajan (98–117 AD). 'There is an 'eight' called the *Leontophoros* which was generally admired for its size and beauty. A hundred men rowed in each file, so that there were 800 men on each side, and on both sides 1600. There were 1200 to fight from the deck and two steersmen'. Casson has taken the provision of two steersmen to indicate that it had, like Ptolemy's 'forty', two hulls. But the information given shows that the problem with this ship would have been not top-heaviness, which two hulls would have met, but excessive length, with 100 men in each file. With 0.9m of length and 0.6m feet of breadth for each oarsman, the rowing area would have been 91m long and the total length 107-114m, the total breadth not less than 9.75m. These hull dimensions are about three times the dimensions of an Athenian 'three' (35m × 3.65m). Steering with steering-oars would have been difficult, and this presumably is the reason for having two steersmen, one to each oar. Height above the waterline need not have been more than 2.7 or 3m as against the 'three's' 2.4m. Compared with Demetrius's monsters, the *Leontophoros* might well have been admired for its elegant lines as well as for its size. What was more important, she was apparently successful in battle. The number of marines she could carry was certainly impressive.

The Roman Imperial Fleets

When Octavian, after learning for himself the hard way the facts of sea-power in his struggle with Sextus Pompeius, gained the victory over Antony's fleet at Actium, his experience would have left him in no doubt that the peace and prosperity resting on commercial expansion which Rome now needed must be built on a solid basis of naval establishments both in Italy and in the provinces. In particular, the food supply of the Roman population must be safeguarded, and lines of communication ensured with the Roman armies in Spain, in Africa and Egypt, in Greece and the Levant, and on the northern river frontiers. Further, the growing commercial routes from Rome to all parts of the Mediterranean had to be protected. Piracy was an endemic evil, which Pompey had eradicated once, but which always threatened to recur. As Augustus Caesar, Octavian put his hand to the task, which was taken up and extended by his successors, of establishing a network of fleets and detached squadrons. Shortly after Actium part of Antony's fleet was stationed at Forum Julii (modern Fréjus) to protect communications with the west. But this base did not rival, either in strength or duration, the two main Italian fleets, the *classes praetoriae*, the more important at Misenum on the northern shore of the Gulf of Naples (from where as commander the elder Pliny set out to succour the victims of the eruption which destroyed Pompeii in AD 79, and to lose his life), the other at Ravenna, facing the perennially lawless Illyrian shore and protecting Roman communications with the Greek mainland. Detached squadrons from these main fleets were assigned to various provincial stations; and as time went on a number of provincial

fleets became established, at Alexandria, at Seleucia (the port of Antioch), at Cyzicus where Nero formed the Black Sea fleet, and at Gesoriacum (modern Boulogne) where Caligula established the *classis Britannica*. There were three river fleets, one on the Rhine and two on the Danube. This comprehensive naval organization lasted until after the Severan emperors. In the succeeding period the growth of piracy and the reappearance in the Roman administration of Italy of the post of prefect of the coastal frontier both suggest that the outlying fleets at any rate had disappeared. During the 3rd century AD the enemies of Rome were able to sail the length and breadth of the Mediterranean unchallenged.

At the time of their greatest strength the praetorian fleets probably amounted to as many as 250 ships each. Eighty-seven names of ships are known in the Misenum fleet. Of these one, the *Ops*, was a 'six' and thus certainly the flagship, and one was a 'five'. The remaining 85 names are divided between ten 'fours', 53 'threes', 13 liburnians, and 9 of unknown rating. Since the liburnians (see p.37 above) are marked in the inscriptions with the figure II it is certain that they were rowed by two files on each side, either with one man to each oar at two levels or with two men to each oar at one level. Fewer names and ratings are known for the Ravenna fleet. Of 33 names two are rated as 'fives', six as 'fours', 20 as 'threes' and three as liburnians. Ships with unknown base are: one 'six', which it is difficult not to regard as the flagship of the Ravenna fleet, three 'fours', 18 'threes' and seven liburnians. The provincial fleets seem to be composed of liburnians with 'threes' as flagships.

Plate 35
(a) Wall painting from
the House of the Priest
Amandus at Pompeii.
AD 54–68.
Photo: Vasari.

(b) Wall painting from
the temple of Isis at
Pompeii. 1st century AD.
From Casson, pl.133.

These lists provide some sort of a background against which we may check the representations of warships which have come down to us from the period of the Empire. The Ostia relief (Pl.31: second half of 1st century BC), like the slightly earlier Calenian bowl (Viereck Pl.17), shows a ship of three levels of oars emerging from oar-ports placed one immediately above the other beneath a side-gangway (*parodos*). The two Pozzuoli reliefs (Pl.32 a and b: 1st BC – 1st AD) show ships with similar oar-systems although the human figures are as so often too grossly out of scale for it to be easy to come to terms with them. One has a side screen and one has not. There are also a number of representations of warships on Pompeian wall paintings of the 1st century AD (Pl.35 b). These ships have decks crowded with armed men and extended by a *parodos* from beneath which clusters of oars emerge. It seems probable that they are similar to the ships on the Ostia and Pozzuoli reliefs and are larger three-level ships, very probably 'sixes'. There is however one ship on a wall painting in the House of the Priest Amandus at Pompeii (Pl.35a: AD 54-68) which is different. There is a railed deck crowded with armed men. The outward curving stanchions supporting the deck are visible, and immediately below these stanchions emerges a file of oars from an outrigger. Below the outrigger two oars of a zygian file are visible and one of a thalamian file. The ship accordingly seems to be a 'three' with an oar-system indentical to that of the Athenian 'threes' as they can be reconstructed (see above Pl.21).

Trajan's column, which belongs to the beginning of the 2nd century AD, shows a number of long ships of the Danube squadron. They are all aphract, and the figures of oarsmen, as those of Trajan and his officers, are even more enormously out-of-scale than usual. Trajan's flagship (Pl.36) is an aphract three-level long ship and thus certainly a 'three'. The remainder are two-level ships, certainly liburnians. The artist appears to have been a landsman. His visible oarsmen row, one man to an oar, in a most unseamanlike way. The uppermost file of the 'three' work their oars, as the upper file of the liburnians do, through the side rails. The absence of a marked outrigger in the 'three' may be a mistake on the artist's part, or it may be due to the difficulty of representing the third dimension in a relief (cf. the Lenormant relief Pl.16 below). In any case if the Trajan's column 'three' is compared with the three-level ship on the Ostia relief (Pl.31) the difference between a 'three' and a 'six' is manifest.

In the 2nd century BC Aelius Aristides claimed that the god Poseidon had been Rome's ally because she had given him a sea clear of battles, and full of merchant ships instead of warships. There were occasions when there were rival contestants for the empire, but only once was the issue decided at sea. The function of the imperial fleets was police work, ensuring the safety of sea communications, and river communications, for the armies and for government and trade.

The larger types of long ship seem gradually to have been abandoned. When Tacitus at the beginning of the second century AD mentions a 'three' in his account of contemporary events, it is usually as a flagship or as employed on some special mission. Dio Cassius, writing of the ships with which Julius Caesar defeated the Veneti off the Loire in 56 BC (xxxix 41), uses a phrase which is revealing for his own time, the beginning of the 3rd century AD. 'Caesar's ships' he says 'tended for the sake of speed to lightness of build, approaching the manner of naval building employed today'. He thus draws a strong contrast between the solidly built polyremes of the civil wars and earlier, the 'fours', 'fives', and 'sixes', and the lightly built long ships of his own day. It is probable too that the considerable seamanlike skill needed for the successful handling in battle of even a 'three' was gradually lost through lack of opportunity to practise it under realistic conditions. When Zosimus, in the 5th century

Plate 36 Detail from Trajan's column showing Trajan's flagship, an aphract trireme. Early 2nd century AD.
Photo: Museum of Classical Archaeology, Cambridge.

AD, describes the final struggle between Constantine and Licinius (in 323), he says that Licinius had collected a fleet of 350 'threes' while Constantine had 200 triacontors (which is no doubt Zosimus' archaistic way of naming liburnians); and that 200 of Licinius' 'threes' were defeated in the narrow waters of the Hellespont by 80 of Constantine's lighter vessels. Ultimately the 'three' became obsolete and the method of

its construction was forgotten. When speaking of the liburnians which the Gothic chief Fravitta employed in the Aegean in AD 400, Zosimus says (V 20 3–4): 'these seem to be not less speedy than pentecontors though far inferior to ships of the 'three' type, the method of construction of the latter having been forgotten many years before'.

Finally Vegetius, in the 5th century, gives an account of the liburnians used in his own time (*de re militari* ii 1). These can be seen to have evolved by the 9th century into the Byzantine dromons which Leo describes (*Tactica* xix 7) in some detail. They are plainly rather larger versions of the two-level pentecontors with which the development of the long ship began in the 8th century BC.

The Round Ships

This narrative began with an account of seafaring in the Mediterranean, whether for war or trade, in the Bronze Age. It was next concerned with the long ship from its appearance on Attic Geometric vases in the eighth century to the end of the Roman Empire. The subject will, finally, be the merchant ship from the end of the Bronze Age, its employment and construction. We have very little information about the construction of the round ship, some notices in Theophrastus about the timber employed and some information deriving from the excavation of a number of merchant ships in recent years. No large space is needed, since the merchant ship seems to have developed very little, except in size, over the centuries. The sources for our knowledge of the period are interested more in the evolution of political and military power than in trade, with the result that the information which we get about the ships in which that trade was carried is correspondingly limited. Nevertheless, the creation of wealth through trade is at the root of political and military power and the events which have provided the framework for the history of the long ship presuppose, what they do not often reveal, a background of busy maritime trading activity throughout the Mediterranean, interrupted from time to time, and for considerable periods, when the sea-routes became insecure through war or piracy, but reviving again with a quick resilience when security was restored.

In the 12th century BC the coast of Syria, from Cilicia to the Egyptian border, was studded with Phoenician cities depending on trade for their livelihood. Ugarit perished about 1150 BC, and when the Egyptian Wen Amon was sent on a mission to obtain ship's timber from the King of Byblos in 1100 he escaped with difficulty from the coastal pirates and found the king unimpressed by the prestige of the Pharaoh that had sent him. From as early as the 10th century Phoenician traders carried the metals mined in the neighbouring territories to points further west. They went via Cyprus to Cythera, where they established the worship of Astarte/Aphrodite, and to the Greek mainland where the traditional Phoenician origins of the Theban royal house and the north Syrian alphabet attest their presence. From there they went to Sicily, then to the opposite African coast in the region of Utica, and then northwards to Sardinia and westwards again to Gades at the mouth of the river Baetis (modern Guadalquivir) and to other trading posts on the African coast beyond the pillars of Hercules. About 800 BC they founded Carthage. Homer and Herodotus knew them as traders and kidnappers.

In Egypt the Phoenicians were established by the 8th century as traders, and their craftsmen are found in the dockyards. But by the end of the 7th century Ionian Greeks, particularly from Miletus, had established a trading post in competition with them at Naucratis in the Delta, where Corinthian and Samian merchants were also to be found. And Greeks began to compete with Phoenicians also as colonizers in the western Mediterranean. Greeks also opened up an area of colonization in the north east, to which the Phoenicians had not penetrated. In Finley's words: 'By the end of the Archaic Age Hellas covered an enormous area, from the north western and southern shores of the Black Sea through western Asia Minor and Greece proper (with the Aegean islands) to much of Sicily and

Southern Italy, then continuing west along both shores of the Mediterranean to Cyrene in Libya and Marseilles and some Spanish coastal sites'. The expansion was not without some opposition. The battle of Alalia in 535 BC off Sardinia between the Phocaeans and a combined fleet of Etruscans and Carthaginians has been mentioned (p.17). Under pressure from the Greeks, Carthaginians seem to have sought fresh horizons outside the Mediterranean. Trade competition between Phoenicians and Greeks may perhaps be seen to have reached its climax and its resolution in the events which terminate the Archaic Age, when the Carthaginian assault on Sicily was repelled by Gelon at the battle of Himera and the Persian fleet, of which the Phoenician naval contingent was the backbone, was defeated at Salamis, both according to tradition on the same day in the late summer of 480 BC. The tradition need not be believed, but it does attest a contemporary feeling that the double threat to the world of Hellas from east and west had a common motive and source.

The Phocaeans are said by Herodotus (I 163 tr.Powell) to have 'practised long seafarings before the other Greeks; and they are the people that shewed the way to the Adriatic and Tyrrhenia and Iberia and Tartessus. And they voyaged not in round ships (strongyloi) but in pentecontors'. He tells how when the Persian Harpagus attacked the Ionian cities in 543 BC 'the Phocaeans launched their pentecontors and set therein their children and their wives and all their furniture... and sailed unto Chios'. These are clearly vessels with considerable space for cargo and passengers in addition to their crews of 25 oarsmen a side. But they were warships because their rams are mentioned later in the account of the battle of Alalia. The fact that Herodotus speaks of making long voyages in pentecontors as a Phocaean peculiarity indicates that round ships were normal for such voyages. When Homer (Od.5 250) refers to a 'broad merchantman' he is meaning the normal round trading ship, like

the 9m ship found off Cape Gelidonya (see above p.12) and the makeshift boat which Odysseus builds in the Odyssey (5 228 ff: see below p.55 ff). The advantage of the round ship for long voyages was that it carried much cargo, was stable in rough weather, had a small crew of three or four, and since it was not beached like the long ship each night could undertake long voyages without intermediate ports of call. The black-figure cup in the British Museum (Pl.15), dated about 510 BC shows two round ships and two two-level pentecontors, the latter towing smaller craft. The painting gives an excellent illustration of the ships of both kinds in which the Greeks of the 7th and 6th centuries carried out their voyages of trade and exploration, and of colonization. The length of the merchant ships on the cup may be estimated very roughly by comparison with the pentecontors, the length of which can be calculated by the fixed distance between the rowlocks (the interscalmium i.e. 0.88m). At deck level the length of the round ships is about 15m (a little less than 50ft) so substantially longer than the Gelidonya ship but just about the same length as the Kyrenia ship (Pl.42 fourth century). M. Jean Rougé's La marine dans l'antiquité (pp.83–7) should be consulted for some sensible remarks about the tonnage of ancient cargo-ships.

The victories of Himera and Salamis ensured that throughout the Mediterranean Greek navies were dominant and hence that Greek trade by sea was in the ascendancy. Massilia and Syracuse in the west and Piraeus in the east became the main Greek commercial centres. Athens depended on the import of corn through Piraeus, mainly from the Hellespont. The ships that brought it were privately chartered and carried about 3000 medimnoi, 150 tons metric. Cargo of this order of magnitude would have been carried by the round ships on the British Museum cup (Pl.15) and by the Kyrenia ship (Pl.42). When Philip of Macedon seized the Black Sea grain fleet in 340 BC it numbered 230 ships of which all but 50 were Athenian. Merchant ships were commonly called *holkades* i.e. towed ships (*GOS* 244–5) in the 5th century, a name which indicated that where a long ship would have used oars in navigation a merchant ship would have been towed. There are occasions in literature when they are towed by oared ships and when they are 'necessarily' accompanied by oared ships (Demosthenes 50 22, Thucydides VI 44[1]). Merchant ships are described as riding at anchor, never as beached as the long ships were. Their customary lead sheathing would have made beaching, in any case, undesirable. Demosthenes speaks of a 20-oared ship which carried 3000 jars of wine (35 18). There are no pictures of such ships surviving from the 4th century BC, but there is a fine Roman mosaic of the 2nd or 3rd century AD at Tébessa in Algeria (Pl.37), which shows a 20-oared ship with a deck cargo of jars (*amphorae*). Another, without a visible cargo and with the main mast lowered, is shown on a mosaic in the Baths at Themetra in Tunisia (p.2). This kind of hybrid long/round ship, which avoided the necessity of towing but could only carry a limited deck cargo since the hold was occupied by a single file of oarsmen on each side, is to be found throughout our period (see below p.55).

Corn and wine were not the only, though they were probably the most frequent, cargoes. 'The Athenians in the first place', says an anonymous Athenian writer of about 430 BC,' by virtue of their command of the sea have formed luxurious tastes through having inter-course with every possible country. Any delicacy in Sicily or Italy or Cyprus or Egypt or Lydia or Pontus or the Peloponnese or other places, all have been brought together in one place by virtue of the command of the sea'. The same author sees Athens getting the raw materials for her naval programme, 'timber from one source, iron from another, copper, flax and wax from yet others'. He also says that Athens

Plate 37 Mosaic in Tébessa Museum, Algeria. Early 4th century AD. From Casson, pl.140.

is able to close the seas to any competitor who does not bring his cargo to her port.

These were the rewards of sea-power for Athens, as seen by a 5th-century writer. But by the end of the next century, when the conquests of Alexander had brought about a fundamental reorientation of power and economic forces, Alexandria and Antioch (through its port Seleucia) had begun to supplant Piraeus as the trading centres of the east Mediterranean. The naval ambitions of the Hellenistic kings, leading to huge and unwieldy ships of war, were matched by similar ventures in merchant ship-building. The *Syracosia*, which carried a cargo of about 2000 metric tons was constructed by Hiero of Syracuse and presented by him to Ptolemy III. This was plainly an exceptional ship and in fact only made a single voyage, from Syracuse to Alexandria (Athenaeus V 206d–209: Casson p.184–186). In the west the rise of Rome, the eventual destruction of Carthage and Rome's conquest of the Greek cities of southern Italy and Sicily, and her growing influence throughout the Mediterranean,

53

produced another reorientation. At the outset Rome had virtually no trading fleet, and her establishment of Delos as a free port and her destruction of Corinth was at first more to the benefit of her Aegean allies than of herself. Her trading interests in the eastern Mediterranean grew however rapidly until rudely checked by Mithradates of Pontus in the early years of the 1st century BC. The Mithradatic wars, the spread of piracy and the struggles for power within the Roman state must have reduced trade to a minimum in the years that followed.

The network of naval power which Augustus established, and the peace and security which ensued, led to an enormous and rapid increase in trading activity of all kinds from Spain to the Cimmerian Bosphorus and the Red Sea. In the eastern Mediterranean Alexandria was now the commercial centre. A large fleet of grain-carriers set off annually in the spring from Alexandria to Ostia, in the brief season before the Etesian winds in mid-July made westward navigation difficult. Trading ships from the coast of Asia Minor would either come south to Alexandria and sail from there to Rome with the grain fleet or take the more northerly route via

Cyprus and Crete. To Alexandria would also come cargoes of silk and spices from India and Ethiopia and beyond via the Red Sea and the Nile waterways. There were grain imports through Ostia also from Sicily and Libya, from where a second grain fleet was organized by Commodus in the last quarter of the 2nd century AD when the supply from Egypt was interrupted. Augustus and his successors took a personal interest in the corn trade and in corn prices, and encouraged that trade in various ways. Claudius, Nero and Trajan took special measures to improve and extend the port of Ostia.

The shortness of the period of favourable winds for the laborious voyage from Alexandria to Ostia put a premium on extra cargo space, and led to an increase in the tonnage of vessels. Large ships were also needed for the transport of the legions and their supplies in the defence of the imperial frontiers. There are a number of representations of these ships, but the constant artistic convention of making the human figures more, often grossly more, than life-size makes the task of estimating their actual dimensions very difficult. What is probably a sizeable cargo ship is often made by this

Plate 39 Mosaic from the Foro delle Corporazioni at Ostia. About AD 200. Photo: Vasari.

convention to look like a dingy (Pl.38). The cargo vessel shown on Trajan's column (Casson p.150) is again a case in point. On the other hand, the cargo ship of the 2nd century AD on a sarcophagus in Beirut (Casson Pl.156) looks substantially larger than the ships, carrying about 150 tons metric, on the British Museum cup (Pl.15), but the reason may be that it shows no human figures. The same is true of the ships on the mosaics at Ostia (Pl.39) and from Themetra in Tunisia (Pl.32). These are round, symmetrically shaped ships, perhaps of the type called *muriophoros*, 'ten-thousand carrier'. The legal texts speak of corn ships of 10000 or 50000 *modii*, i.e. 90 or 450 metric tons. The big ships we see are likely to be the latter, so that whatever the 10000 was the *muriophoros* carried it was probably not *modii*.

As we have seen (pp. 10, 53), there was also a type of cargo carrier which had its cargo on deck leaving the hold for a file of oarsmen on both sides. This type also has a projecting forefoot. The most striking example of many is the ship on the 2nd or 3rd century mosaic from Tébessa (Pl.37) showing a 20-oared ship with a wide deck supported on stanchions beneath which a single file of ten oars emerges, while on deck there is a tightly-packed cargo of *amphorae*. That cargo carriers with projecting forefoot were common is shown by the frequency with which they appear on the mosaics which decorated the floors of the offices surrounding the Courtyard of the Corporations at Ostia (Pl.40). A symmetrical ship is often paired with an asymmetrical one. The reasons for the variation can only be guessed at. Perhaps the oared ship protected, and when necessary towed, the other. There is no indication that the asymmetrical cargo ships were *naves aeratae* i.e. were equipped with a metal ram. The big cargo ships on the mosaics in the Baths at Themetra (Pl.41) were asymmetrical. The forefoot, as in many of the ships on the contemporary Althiburus mosaic in the Musée Bardo at Tunis, is certainly not offensive but structural, and

seems to be a feature of ships which normally were rowed i.e. galleys and oared merchantmen or of ships which could be rowed but seldom were, i.e. the bigger asymmetrical merchant ships (see p.10 above).

The construction of the round ships

An account of the construction of merchant ships must begin with the description in Homer (*Odyssey* 5 243–261) of the boat which Odysseus built on Calypso's island. Calypso first tells Odysseus 'where tall trees grow, alder and poplar and pine, dry long ago, well seasoned'. He then set to, cutting the planks, and quickly got on with the job. He dragged out twenty felled trees, and 'adzed them with the bronze. He cleverly planed them and made them straight to the line'. 'Then Calypso brought drills and he bored holes in all the planks and fitted them to each other. He hammered the boat together with *gomphoi* and *harmoniai*. As broad an *edaphos* of a wide merchantman as a man skilled in carpentry will round out (*tornosetai*), so broad an *edaphos* did Odysseus fashion for his wide boat'. The word *gomphoi* may be taken to mean the

Plate 40 Mosaic from the Foro delle Corporazioni at Ostia. About AD 200. Photo: Vasari.

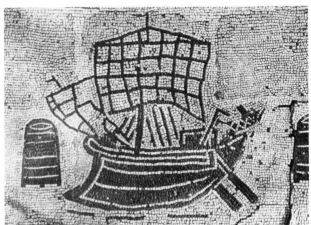

Plate 41 Mosaic from the Baths at Themetra (nr Sousse, Tunisia). About the middle of the third century AD. After L.Foucher *op. cit.* fig.5.

pegs, dowels or trenails by which the mortise and tenon joints were secured. It may also mean the tenons themselves. The word *edaphos* means the whole rounded hull of the vessel, which is plainly no raft as used to be supposed, but a complete, if makeshift, boat. The word *tornosetai* emphasises the rounding of the hull. The Kyrenia ship (Pl.42) was about 12m long and 5m broad and had about 12 planking strakes and wales on each side of the keel. The Cape Gelidonya Bronze Age ship (p.12, above) was about 9m (30ft) long and on the basis of the measurements of the Kyrenia ship would have been 3.35m broad. Made of twenty 9m planks Odysseus' boat would have closely resembled the Cape Gelidonya ship in size. The latter, unlike the Kyrenia ship, probably had no keel. In both wrecks, as in the boat of Odysseus, the hull planking was joined edge-to-edge by dowel, mortise and tenon.

It is obviously unwise to infer too much from two isolated wrecks. Nevertheless the fact that the earlier wreck had no keel while the later wreck had one may be significant, since there is no mention of a keel in the boat of Odysseus, nor is there a keel in the earliest preserved vessel, the Cheops ship of *ca.*2650BC. Herodotus, in the 5th century BC, writes about the construction of cargo-carrying ships in Egypt at his time (II 96): 'their ships for carrying cargo are made of acantha... From this acantha then they cut timbers of two cubits length, and assemble them like bricks using the following method of ship-building. They make courses of planking around long, close-set pegs (*gomphoi*: here certainly tenons); and when they build ships in this way they stretch frames over the surface of (*epipolēs*) the planks. They use no *nomeis*, and reinforce the timbers from within with *byblos* (papyrus). They make one rudder oar and this is passed through the keel. The mast is of acantha and the sails of *byblos*.' The publication of details of the Cheops ship by Landström throws light on this passage in two places. The hull timbers of the nearly flat bottom of the ship are joined edge-to-edge by mortice and tenon; and then cords are passed through pairs of holes in each plank which make a V shaped passage, thus reinforcing the mortice and tenon joint. It looks therefore as if the sentence in Herodotus generally translated: 'they caulked the seams from within with *byblos*' may refer instead to the use of cords, for which *byblos* was the normal material (*GOS* p.57), to reinforce the joints as in the Cheops ship. Caulking in any case is better carried out from outside the hull. In the second place, when Herodotus says: 'they stretch *zuga* over the surface of the planks', these *zuga* have been taken to mean thwarts, the usual meaning of the word in this context. However, the Egyptian ships described are cargo-carriers, not long ships, and thwarts would have been as few as possible. Furthermore, the word *epipolēs* means 'over the surface of (and touching) the planks'. It seems plain then that these *zuga* are not thwarts but frames, and are exactly illustrated in the Cheops ship. The fact that the latter is about 2000 years earlier than the ships Herodotus describes should not make the comparison less useful and enlightening. Methods of ship-building, where the materials remain the same, are notoriously unchanging.

In describing the construction of the ship's hull Herodotus mentions no keel, but he does mention a keel when he goes on to describe the rudder mounting. Single rudders mounted in a groove or fork in the stern, in contrast to the side-slung rudders normal in the Mediterranean, are noticeable in the smaller Egyptian ships of the Middle and New kingdom (Landström pp.75 ff, 122 ff), which are almost certainly keelless. It seems that Herodotus is speaking loosely and means no more than that the rudder was mounted on the middle line. In any case the keel proper could hardly be said to continue to a height in the stern such that the rudder could pass through it. If that is so, we may regard the type of keelless shell-constructed cargo ships built in Egypt from the 3rd millennium BC to the time of Herodotus as the proto-type of the Cape Gelidonya ship and of the boat which Homer describes as built by Odysseus.

After completing the hull Odysseus turns to the superstructure, the *ikria*, i.e. the raised poop where the helmsman and the important passengers sat (*GOS* pp.47–8). Such a poop is a noticeable feature of long ships (see Pl.6, 9, 11, 12). The side view shows uprights and a longitudinal rail, together forming a short fence on each side of a platform or seat on which the helmsman sits. So Odysseus 'sets up and fashions the *ikria*, fitting it with many uprights, and completes it with long *epēnkenides*.' The meaning of *epēnkenides* depends on what is thought to be the object of the verb 'completes', the boat as a whole or the *ikria*. The answer must be that the poet is still thinking of the *ikria*, which would certainly need more than uprights to complete it. In the pictures mentioned there are longitudinal rails also, and what is more they touch the helmsman's elbows. Now things 'at the elbow' is just what the word *epēnkenides* can mean. Interpreters who

Plate 42 The Kyrenia Ship. 4th century BC. Photograph by courtesy of Professor M.L.Katzev.

have taken the object of 'completes' as the boat, have identified the *epēnkenides* as e.g. 'long planks bolted to the top of the ribs'. But if we are to take it so, since the word derives from *ankōn* 'an elbow', it is more likely to denote something bent, e.g. 'knees' to carry the upper planking. Oared long ships also have *ikria* in the bow (see Pl.7a and b), but cargo ships have them only in the stern (cf. the model cargo ship dating from the 6th century BC illustrated in Casson pl.94). Odysseus needs one there 'high to carry him over the misty sea'.

Odysseus also equips his boat with wattle screens to keep out the spray, and 'spreads much brushwood'. The latter presents a momentary puzzle. Brushwood was found in the Gelidonya wreck and in others. Since it occurs under the cargo and in the case of the Gelidonya wreck was specially cut to fit, Bass's suggestion seems plausible that it is dunnage, a springy layer to protect the cargo and the planking also from damage in rough weather. Odysseus however had no cargo in prospect. This detail confirms what is now becoming accepted that Homer is describing the construction of a cargo vessel irrespective of the particular context.

The 5th and 4th century wrecks of merchantmen have keels, and hulls built up of planks edge-joined by dowels, mortise and tenon. To this shell of planks and wales are added on the inside half-frames alternating with futtocks and floor timbers. A particularly well preserved example of this kind of construction is the wreck at La Madrague de Giens (Var) in France (front cover). The whole is sheathed in lead, at any rate below the waterline, over some kind of woven material. These features are found in wrecks of merchantmen continuously until the 7th century AD.

There is a hint however that the shell method of construction was not the only one in the 5th century BC. Herodotus (I 194) describes the building of coracles on the Euphrates by the erection of a frame of *nomeis* and then covering the frame with hides, and in the description of the Egyptian method of building cargo ships, which we have noticed, he says; 'they use no *nomeis*'. Lucien Basch has rightly interpreted *nomeis* as 'active' frames, regulators, making up a framework to which the skin subsequently applied is made to conform, as opposed to the passive framework subsequently added in the shell method. Now the fact that there was a word with the meaning which Herodotus requires, and that he denies that the Egyptians used these members for their cargo ships suggest that active frames were sometimes employed in Greece in his time. The isolated case of the Euphrates coracles would not be enough. But this is the only hint we have. Alternatively, of course, active frames could have been used for the upper strakes, passive for the lower.

The fact that cargo ships were normally kept afloat and not beached or hauled ashore would have made them particularly susceptible to worm. Hence the lead sheathing, the additional weight of which would, in a sailing ship, have been useful as ballast. Ballast was found in the Bronze Age merchantman and has been suspected in the Mahdia wreck (probably 1st century AD). There are references to it in the literature of the 5th and 4th century BC and of the 1st century AD, which indicate that its use was recognized as a stabilizing factor in rough weather. It is of course inconceivable that long ships employed ballast, seeing that they were built as light as possible and were normally and regularly beached and hauled ashore. They were sometimes even hauled over isthmuses and the necks of promontories (Thuc. IV 8²). If, as has been reported, the Punic ship excavated at Lilybaeum (modern Marsala) (Pl.25) was in ballast when she sank, the conclusion must be either that she was a merchantman of the oared asymmetrical type (see Pl.41) noticed above or that if a warship she was empty and therefore in need of ballast under tow.

Index

THE SHIP

The first four titles in this major series of ten books on the development of the ship are: 2. *Long Ships and Round Ships: Warfare and Trade in the Mediterranean, 3000 BC–500 AD*, by John Morrison; 5. *Steam Tramps and Cargo Liners: 1850–1950*, by Robin Craig; 8. *Steam, Steel and Torpedoes: The Warship in the 19th Century*, by David Lyon; and 9. *Dreadnought to Nuclear Submarine*, by Antony Preston.

The remaining six books, which are to be published 1980–1981, will cover: 1. Ships in the ancient world outside the Mediterranean and in the medieval world in Europe (to the 15th century), by Sean McGrail; 3. The ship, from *c.*1550–*c.*1700 (including Mediterranean, Arab World, China, America); 4. The ship from *c.*1700–*c.*1820 (including Mediterranean, Arab World, China, America), both by Alan McGowan; 6. Merchant Steamships (passenger vessels), 1850–1970, by John Maber; 7. Merchant Sail of the 19th Century, by Basil Greenhill; and 10. The Revolution in Merchant Shipping, 1950–1980, by Ewan Corlett.

All titles in *The Ship* series are available from:

HER MAJESTY'S STATIONERY OFFICE
Government Bookshops
49 High Holborn, London WC1V 6HB
13a Castle Street, Edinburgh EH2 3AR
41 The Hayes, Cardiff CF1 1JW
Brazennose Street, Manchester M60 8AS
Southey House, Wine Street, Bristol BS1 2BQ
258 Broad Street, Birmingham B1 2HE
80 Chichester Street, Belfast BT1 4JY
Government publications are also available through booksellers

The full range of Museum publications is displayed and sold at
National Maritime Museum
Greenwich

Obtainable in the United States of America from Pendragon House Inc.
2595 East Bayshore Road
Palo Alto
California 94303

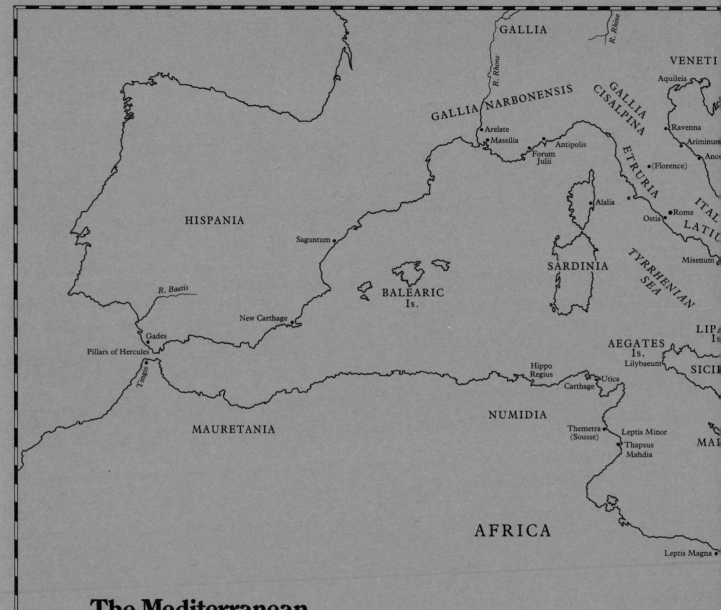

GALLIA

R. Rhine

VENETI

Aquileia

R. Rhone

GALLIA NARBONENSIS

GALLIA CISALPINA

Ravenna

Ariminum

Ance

Arelate

(Florence)

Massilia

ETRURIA

Antipolis

Forum
Julii

ITAL

Alalia

Rome

HISPANIA

Ostia

LATIU

Saguntum

Misenum

SARDINIA

TYRRHENIAN SEA

R. Baetis

BALEARIC
Is.

New Carthage

AEGATES
Is.

LIP
Is.

Gades

Lilybaeum

SICIL

Pillars of Hercules

Hippo
Regius

Tingis

Utica

Carthage

NUMIDIA

MAURETANIA

Themetra
(Sousse)

Leptis Minor

MAI

Thapsus
Mahdia

AFRICA

Leptis Magna

The Mediterranean

0   100 miles